SARAH KOFMAN'S CORPUS

SUNY series in Gender Theory
Tina Chanter, editor

SARAH KOFMAN'S CORPUS

Edited by

Tina Chanter
and
Pleshette DeArmitt

State University of New York Press

Published by
State University of New York Press, Albany

Printed in the United States of America

Cover cartoon entitled Vive l'Armee! by Jules Hérault.

For information, contact State University of New York Press, Albany, NY
www.sunypress.edu

Production by Diane Ganeles
Marketing by Anne M. Valentine

Library of Congress Cataloging-in-Publication Data

Sarah Kofman's corpus / edited by Tina Chanter and Pleshette DeArmitt.
p. cm. — (SUNY series in gender theory)
Includes bibliographical references and index.
ISBN 978-0-7914-7267-5 (hardcover : alk. paper)
ISBN 978-0-7914-7268-2 (pbk. : alk. paper)
1. Kofman, Sarah. I. Chanter, Tina, 1960– II. DeArmitt, Pleshette, 1967–

B2430.K644S27 2007
194—dc22

2007001776

10 9 8 7 6 5 4 3 2 1

Contents

Acknowledgments

This collection on the work of Sarah Kofman developed out of a conference, "Reading Sarah Kofman's Corpus," which took place at DePaul University on October 12, 2001, thanks to the generous support of the Philosophy Department and the University Research Council. The editors of this collection are also grateful to the following people for their assistance in the preparation of the manuscript: Penelope Deutscher, Mary Jo Minerich, Heather Rakes, David Ritchie, Elizabeth Rottenberg, and Kas Saghafi, as well as Wyatt Benner, Jane Bunker, and Diane Ganeles at SUNY Press.

INTRODUCTION

The Lifework of Sarah Kofman

PLESHETTE DeARMITT

> What interests me in Sarah's work, and what knitted much of the friendship between us, is this manner of relating "works" to "life," rather than the converse.... That writing relates to life, and relates it, does not mean the absence of thought nor even its secondary importance. It means that thought does not begin without this gesture of writing and also that, just as it is transmitted by it, so thought ends up with this gesture. But also that "thought," finally, is caught up in life and relates to it, ending in it and therefore capable of ending it: there is no life after thought. A life of thought is perhaps a life that does not already live enough, or that lives too much, or again, quite simply, it is a life that attests itself, inscribing that it took place.
>
> —Jean-Luc Nancy

It is difficult, indeed impossible, to discuss Kofman's vast interdisciplinary corpus, which includes nearly thirty books and numerous articles on philosophical, psychoanalytic, literary, feminist, and Jewish subjects, without telling Kofman's own story. Of course, Kofman would have rightly resisted the reduction of her sophisticated and complex body of work, which treats thinkers and writers as diverse as Empedocles and Plato, Diderot and Nerval, Comte and Kant, and Blanchot and Derrida to mere biography. In fact, she insisted that her own life-narrative, her own biography, can and should be found in her bibliography. Perhaps, this declaration is not so much a gesture of self-effacing modesty or of the impulse to reduce the life of the thinker to his or her work; rather, as Nancy argues, Kofman's writing, her extensive bibliography, is itself a profound attestation to life, to a life, to her life. Although Nancy is correct to say that Kofman, who saw herself as a philosopher first and foremost, related "works" to "life," perhaps he oversimplifies the matter. Kofman, an incisive reader of Nietzsche and Freud, "whose bodies of work," Derrida claims, "she had read ... [l]ike no one else in this century" (Derrida 1997, 137) and to whom she devoted over ten books, developed, as the chapters in this collection show, a new form of textual analysis, one in which philosophy and psychoanalysis mingle together and the conceptual and the biographical cannot be separated.

Although Kofman's readings always attend to the desires and lives of authors, she claims, as Nancy points out, that "it is not a question of my attempting . . . to reduce philosophy to pathology or system to biography. It is rather a certain relationship of system to life which interests me: to see, not what work *owes* to life but what the work *brings* to life" (Nancy 1999, viii). Nonetheless, Kofman was fascinated by the question of autobiography from the beginning to the end of her career, ranging from *Autobiogriffures* (1989a), a reading of Hoffmann's *Cat Murr*, to *Explosion I* (1992), an interpretation of Nietzsche's *Ecce Homo*. In her later works, Kofman pays increasing attention to the writing of her own life and publishes more explicitly autobiographical texts, from several short essays (Collin and Proust 1997) to two starkly different book-length autobiographies.[1] The first work, *Smothered Words*, which is more theoretical in nature, tries to give voice to the unspeakable experience of the Holocaust by juxtaposing readings of several *récits* by Blanchot, including "The Idyll," and Antelme's *The Human Race* with brief, almost "neutral," accounts of her father's deportation to Drancy in 1942 and his subsequent death at Auschwitz. Her own ruptured life-narrative is addressed once again, one final time, in her haunting work, *Rue Ordener, rue Labat*, in which she provides an account of her childhood and adolescence as a Holocaust survivor in France.

Sarah Kofman's Corpus takes seriously the lessons that Kofman's rich body of work teaches us, among them that the work and life of a thinker are inextricably bound together. Thus, each of the essays in this collection navigates this complex economy of thought and desire, of the book and the body, of the corpus and the corpse. The provocative and in-depth analyses offered by each author in this collection explores and expounds upon the central themes—art, affirmation, laughter, aporia, the intolerable, Jewishness, and femininity—that link together Kofman's oeuvre. At the same time as clarifying and deepening our understanding of the essential motifs and ideas in Kofman's writings, this collection sketches a portrait, even begins a biography, of a thinker who was so many things—affirmative, contrary, playful, profound, duplicitous, nuanced, fiery, and determined.

Despite the awe-inspiring breadth and depth of Kofman's corpus, her work has not been widely commented upon in the English-speaking world and, hence, has not been adequately read and studied by Anglophone audiences.[2] Thus this collection brings together Kofman scholars and translators, from various disciplines such as French and German literature, philosophy, and Women's Studies, who are dedicated to the development of "Kofman studies."

This collection aims to consolidate Kofman's reputation as a philosopher whose originality, range, and verve stand as exemplary. It is to be hoped that the chapters that constitute this particular body of writing will open the way for further translations and studies of Kofman's corpus.

In part 1 of the book, "Art, Affirmation and Laughter," the relationship between the economy of life and work is broached through Kofman's analyses of art. Duncan Large, Pleshette DeArmitt and Ann Smock find in Kofman's writing not only a thought that affirms the uniqueness of the work of art but also a thought that transforms itself into an art of affirmation. In the book's first chapter, Large details how the visual arts and "the question of art" in general preoccupied Sarah Kofman throughout her career—from her first book, on Freud's aesthetics (*The Childhood of Art*), to her last, unfinished essay on Rembrandt ("Conjuring Death: Remarks on *The Anatomy Lesson of Doctor Nicolas Tulp*"). Large's chapter focuses in particular on Kofman's *Mélancolie de l'art* and more broadly addresses the issues at stake in her aesthetic writings, by locating them at the intersection of psychoanalysis, deconstruction, and Nietzschean affirmation. Large argues that for Kofman philosophical aesthetics—Platonic, Hegelian, Heideggerian—is a "garrulous" discourse that interrogates the art object only in order to sublate it. The mirror of speculative textuality serves to shield philosophy from the mortifying or maddening potential of the Medusa-like image, even though any attempted denegation of its troubling, uncanny potency is bound to fail.

In *Mélancolie de l'art*, Kofman discusses Diderot's analysis of a portrait by Greuze and develops her own Freudian interpretation of it, which she pushes to the breaking point ("beauty is in mourning for philosophy"), before mimicking Diderot and turning dialogically on the over-elaborated speculation of her own discourse. The caesura thus created is the space of indeterminacy, madness, and play—precisely the space that will be occupied and exploited by the non-mimetic art of modernity (Kandinsky, Magritte, Bacon), the "stifled eloquence" of which Kofman celebrates in the final section of her essay. Large concludes that for Kofman the gap between the figurative and discursive orders cannot be filled, even by a concept as ingenious as "the melancholy of art." "The question of art," as she formulates it—like "the question of woman"—has no definitive, univocal answer, but functions instead as a disruptive operation, unsettling any theoretical discourse that would master it—including, ultimately, Kofman's own.

In the following chapter, DeArmitt also undertakes to clarify Kofman's demystification of art and beauty by specifically examining art's cathartic or pharmaceutical function. She does so by offering a close reading of a dense passage by Kofman that appears on the back cover of *Mélancolie de l'art*, a passage that DeArmitt reads as a reformulation of Freud's "On Transience." DeArmitt, first, turns to *L'imposture de la beauté* to analyze the role of narcissism in the aesthetic experience; to further comprehend the salutary nature of art, she examines Kofman's reworking of the categories of the Apollonian and Dionysian in her 1979 text *Nietzsche et la scène philosophique*. There, Kofman reveals the duplicitous nature of beauty's Apollonian mask, which is both the face of and a veil over the Dionysian. Dionysus is, on Kofman's reading, a figure of that which is utterly unbearable to behold or, as she describes it, "the intolerable." Thus, the beauty, or the Apollonian, that renders the intolerable tolerable is already self-divided, harboring its double within itself.

Nonetheless, Kofman recognizes that the mask of beauty that is worn by all works of art, as they transform intolerable "realities" into tolerable "illusions," offers the spectator the reassuring face of eternity, that is, the illusion of immortality. The artistic image, be it of Medusa's head or a cadaver on the dissection table, has the power of occultation, bringing about "forgetting" or, in psychoanalytic language, "repression." Although Kofman will call for art to break with its "desire for eternity," a call that simultaneously demands mourning and melancholy (the impossibility of mourning), she does not negate the illusion of art and beauty, but, as DeArmitt argues, affirms another light, which still possesses pharmaceutical powers and provides serenity without salvation.

In the final chapter of part 1, Smock addresses the duplicitous and affirmative power of laughter and wit in the writings of Kofman. This chapter is inspired by Kofman's pleasure in jokes and word-play of all kinds. On the one hand, it links this delight of hers to an irreverent determination to get the better of the authorities, to outdo the censors, to get around everyone and everything that is liable to hem you in and ultimately defeat you, including death. On the other hand, the chapter connects Kofman's love of jokes to her engagement in a double game, played on two terrains at once. For she found herself hemmed in on many fronts and was always inventing and borrowing expedients. Unwilling to lament her fate, Kofman did not believe there was a way out, ultimately, and was disinclined to be consoled by illusions. Unwilling to believe, then, or not believe—unwilling to be duped or disenchanted either—she played on the terrain of confidence and on the terrain of despair, uncompromisingly.

Smock cleverly demonstrates how Kofman cultivated the love of illusions, as only those strong enough to do without them can. Jokes, as Freud emphasized, are Janus-faced, and those best suited to joking are double themselves: both exuding self-confidence and willing to turn their humor on themselves. Humor guarantees a happily imperturbable subject-position, which it simultaneously reveals to be non-existent. Thus it muddies up the simple oppositions between victory and defeat, mastery and abjection; it dwells gaily in despair. By the same token, humor is an ally of Eros, the intermediary and thus daimonic being whom Kofman describes in *Comment s'en sortir?* as neither rich nor poor, male nor female, foolish nor wise, and as foreign to the logic of identity—a devilish philosopher, not unlike Kofman.

Although all the readings of Kofman in this collection negotiate the relationship between work and life, the essays in part 2, "Philosophical Fires: Autobiography, Femininity, and Jewishness," explore in depth the relationship between philosophy and autobiography. In the opening essay of part 2, Naas reveals Kofman to be an exemplary reader and teacher of Plato's work, despite the fact that Kofman wrote only one short book and a handful of texts on Plato. Naas' essay examines the importance of Kofman's work on Plato not only for Plato scholarship, but also for an understanding of Kofman's entire oeuvre. His essay begins with a close reading of Kofman's *Comment s'en sortir?* in order to show that Kofman's thesis concerning the way in which Plato had to use the very elements he wished to overcome in order to establish philosophy—elements such as sophistry, myth, and aporia—constitutes a paradigm for what Kofman believes philosophy has done and must continue to do. So as to "make the intolerable tolerable"—a phrase Naas follows from *Comment s'en sortir?* through many of Kofman's most important works—philosophy cannot help but adopt a kind of "fire wall" strategy to define and affirm itself; that is, in order to exclude certain discourses it must use even more sophisticated forms of those discourses to protect itself effectively from their influence. What is intolerable to philosophy is thus never simply excluded from it, but is always transformed and integrated, displaced and incorporated, in a word, repressed.

It is through this notion of repression that Naas turns, in the final part of his essay, to an interpretation of Kofman's appendix to *Comment s'en sortir?*, which is a short dream and dream analysis simply entitled "Nightmare." This autobiographical appendix, Naas contends, indicates that the entire text needs to be reread "autobiographically," that is, as a displacement of Kofman's "family scene" onto the family scene she spends most of the book interpreting: Socrates' account of Diotima's speech about the origins of Eros in the *Symposium*. On the basis of this, Naas suggests that almost all of Kofman's work can be read as the inevitable reflection or displacement of her own complex family scene (which includes a father arrested and deported by the Nazis, two mothers—one Jewish, one Christian—competing for Sarah's loyalty and affection, and a number of sibling rivalries). He concludes by demonstrating that as late as her two volumes on Nietzsche's *Ecce Homo* published in the early 1990s, Kofman is attempting to develop a novel form of philosophical autobiography, which explains why and how both philosophy and those who practice it must work to "make the intolerable tolerable."

In the fifth chapter, Schrift examines the final of Sarah Kofman's five books on Nietzsche, entitled *Le mépris des Juifs: Nietzsche, les Juifs, l'antisémitisme*.

Schrift discusses and critically assesses Kofman's defense of Nietzsche against the charge of anti-Semitism. While he agrees with Kofman that Nietzsche was not the *reichsdeutsch* anti-Semite that his sister and others wanted him to be, and that too many readers on both sides of the English Channel have thought him to be, Schrift is not persuaded by Kofman's account that "in order for Nietzsche to become-Nietzsche, he had to become a Jew." She may be correct in suggesting that ultimately Nietzsche becomes who and what he is by settling accounts, once and for all, "with the Germany of the Reich, with his mother and his sister, and with the paternal substitutes who had been, among others, Wagner and Schopenhauer." And she may be right as well to conclude that to settle these accounts meant settling accounts with the anti-Semitism that was perhaps their central unifying feature. Yet, Schrift remains skeptical of Kofman's general conclusion that Nietzsche's anti-Semitism can be regarded as a youthful excess that he eventually outgrew. Instead, Schrift offers several alternatives to this conclusion that suggest that while Nietzsche is not the racist anti-Semite that the Nazi ideologists tried to make him out to be, it is a mistake to read Nietzsche's anti-anti-Semitism as pro- or philo-Semitism.

Chapter 6 further develops the Jewish question that is central to Kofman's oeuvre. Tina Chanter examines the relationship between Kofman's earlier, more scholarly work on Freud and her later, more autobiographical and literary works, in which she talks about, among other things, her father, who died at Auschwitz. In doing so, Chanter traces the motif of homosexuality through Kofman works (especially those on Freud) and suggests that it is connected in a fundamental way to the feminine and Judaism. Freud, in an essay on the acquisition of fire, makes some striking claims about homosexuality, which also inform key texts such as *Civilization and Its Discontents*. This little read essay, "The Acquisition and Control of Fire," together with some other better-known texts, such as Freud's case history of Dora, and his essay on the uncanny, form some of the reference points for this paper. Other reference points include Kofman's autobiographical texts—*Rue Ordener, rue Labat* and *Smothered Words*. In the spirit of Kofman's own manner of writing and philosophizing, Chanter perceptively relates Kofman's own work to her life following through the ways in which Kofman's writing reflects the coping strategies she adopted in order to deal not only with the death of her father but also with the feelings that arose in relation to the substitute mother she was granted as a result of her wartime evacuation. The loss of Kofman's father, together with the uncanny doubling of her mother, finds an echo in the religio-political circumstances that shaped both Kofman's life, and her writing. Chanter follows through a suggestion she finds in Kofman's last works, works that can be read as a mourning of her father. The scholarly mastery of Kofman's earlier work gives way to a writing that flows more freely, a style that is no less artful for being less, strictly speaking, philosophical. In her autobiographical works,

Kofman's writing finally comes into its own. It is as if she lets go of the intensely masterful, scholarly style that marks her earlier work, a letting go that would not be what it is without the care and discipline of that mastery, a release that stands in tension with her more overtly philosophical style. A breaking through of death, one might say. This breakthrough is intimately connected, in Chanter's reading, with the enigma of homosexuality that Kofman writes into her life, as if its passing, too, were being mourned.

In the final essay of the collection, Deutscher also investigates the question of woman and femininity in Sarah Kofman's corpus. Deutscher traces the term "becoming-woman" in Kofman's writings from her book on Comte (*Aberrations*), two years after Deleuze's discussion of becoming-woman in his interviews with Claire Parnet, Kofman employs the term in her subsequent interpretations of Rousseau, Freud, Sartre, and Diderot, among others. Unlike many of the other concepts she transformed, this term was not attributed to another philosopher (one might have expected an acknowledgment to Deleuze) until an interview Kofman gave in 1991, in which she suggested that the term "becoming-woman" had actually been inspired by Simone de Beauvoir's concept that "one is not born a woman, one becomes one." Kofman, a former student of Deleuze, was rerouting a term uniquely associated with the work of Deleuze and Guattari to Beauvoir—giving the latter a theoretical place in association with Nietzche, Derrida, Deleuze etc. Kofman neither offers a close reading of Beauvoir nor Deleuze, nor stages an intersection of their work, rather she proposes a problematic that arises only once a term belonging to the one is attributed to the other.

Deutscher's chapter then looks at Kofman's depictions of the becoming-woman of Sartre, Rousseau, Comte and Freud. The philosophers interpreted by Kofman love the women with whom they cannot, though do, identify, as they try to hold onto rigid gender opposition, as they are afraid of (and desirous of) becoming women. Becoming-woman, Kofman argues, nonetheless does take place. Further, Deutscher argues that Kofman's alliance with Beauvoir highlights her interest in what is being transformed in these processes of becoming: not just Rousseau, Comte, Freud or Sartre, that is, not only in the men who become women. She is interested in the transformation of the "woman" in her becoming woman. The notion of woman becomes displaced amongst the diverse and inconsistent resonances of being modest, seductive, frivolous, fertilizable, manipulable, maternal, appropriative of man's place, narcissistically self-sufficient, self-protective, penis envying, bourgeois, missed, mourned, regretted, sickly, mad, degraded, death-like, stimulating, rejuvenating, moral, tender. In conclusion, Deutscher claims that for Kofman we are all, women and men, becoming-woman.

Notes

1. For two biographical sources on Kofman, see Saghafi 2001, 2003, and DeArmitt 2006.

2. See, however, Deutscher and Oliver 1999.

PART I

Art, Affirmation, and Laughter

CHAPTER 1

"The Question of Art": Sarah Kofman's Aesthetics

DUNCAN LARGE

This chapter focuses on an area of Kofman's work that has otherwise been little discussed so far (and that, in particular, is poorly served by the available English translations of her work), but that nevertheless represents a large set of concerns, namely what one might call her enduring fascination with questions of visuality and its representations, with the relation between image and text, beauty and the imposture of beauty, art and its theorization in philosophical aesthetics—the nexus of philosophy, psychoanalysis, and aesthetics in her work.

In *Nietzsche and Metaphor*, Kofman argues persuasively that Nietzsche's visual metaphors are deliberately relativized—as part of his attack on the "speculative" tradition in philosophy generally—so as to privilege the manifold sensorium that is the body as a whole. "Perspectivism" notwithstanding, Kofman argues here that the sense of vision in Nietzsche does not dominate a "hierarchy of the senses," but finds its place rather among a peer group to which it is, at times, even strategically subordinated (1993b, 105–8). Nietzsche does claim, after all, that his genius is in his nostrils (Nietzsche 1992, 96). This seems to me the point at which Kofman herself was at greatest variance from this otherwise favored thinker, for she—to borrow Goethe's self-description—was an *Augenmensch* ("eye-person"), as anyone who had personal contact with her will know. She chose the cover illustrations for her books with great care and corresponded, by preference, on picture postcards, urging her reader—even there—to consider the relation between recto and verso, text and image. When her twin books on Nietzsche's *Ecce homo* appeared, *Explosion I* (1992) and *Explosion II* (1993c); I wrote a review article and called it "Double 'Whaam!,'" alluding to the Roy Lichtenstein painting (Large 1995). It was typical of Kofman that, when I sent her the piece, she was prompted to browse through some catalogs of Lichtenstein's work and reported with delight on encountering two further paintings of his that neither of us had known before, called "Explosion I" and "Explosion II." She herself was no mean artist: a number of her books and articles were published with her own illustrations, and a first exhibition of her work was mounted in Paris shortly before her death in 1994.[1]

Kofman's personal preoccupations inevitably informed her publications—indeed, with the possible exception, ironically enough, of *Aberrations*, her book on Auguste Comte (1978), she wrote only about subjects to which she was passionately committed (in the conclusion to *Explosion II* she goes so far as to declare her *love* for Nietzsche) (1993c, 371). The visual arts in particular, and "the question of art" in general, were such subjects; more than that, they concerned her from first to last, from her first book, *L'enfance de l'art* (1970), translated as *The Childhood of Art* (1988b), to her very last productions. The late autobiographical text *Rue Ordener, rue Labat* (1996) breaks off from its otherwise unselfconscious, unreflexive mode of narration only twice, to discuss Hitchcock and Leonardo da Vinci. Significantly, the essays collected in her last, posthumous, collection entitled *L'imposture de la beauté* (*The Imposture of Beauty*, 1995a), included not only the title essay, on Wilde's *The Picture of Dorian Gray*, but also shorter pieces on Hitchcock, again, and Victor Sjörström, and her last work of all was the uncollected torso of an essay on Rembrandt's *Anatomy Lesson*, "La mort conjurée" (Conjuring Death) which, with supreme irony, was left unfinished at her own death and published posthumously, still largely in note form (1995b). For Kofman, "the question of art" was one of those unanswered and unanswerable questions to which she returned continually—one might say even compulsively—over the course of her career. In her discussions of art the stakes are invariably high; for Kofman (pace Laplanche) it will always be a question of life and death in aesthetic analysis (see Laplanche 1976).

The text on which I want to focus in what follows is the essay entitled "La mélancolie de l'art" (The Melancholy of Art), which was published initially in 1980 as Kofman's contribution to an edited collection and then became, five years later, the title essay in her own collection *Mélancolie de l'art*.[2] Neither her collection as a whole nor this title essay in particular has yet been translated into English, which perhaps goes some way to explaining the relative lack of interest in Kofman's aesthetic inquiry in the "Anglo-Saxon" world so far, and is one reason why I want to concentrate on it. Another is indicated by the subtitle of the collection for which she originally wrote it, *Matériaux pour un enseignement* (Teaching Materials). The essay, then, represents a summation of Kofman's work on aesthetics to this point—roughly speaking, halfway through her philosophical career, as it would turn out—encapsulated in a relatively brief compass (only just over twenty pages even in the revised, slightly extended later version), for propaedeutic purposes. It represents, moreover, the point at which—as Deleuze said of his 1968 works *Difference and Repetition* and *Logic of Sense*—Kofman began writing on art "more on her own account."[3] Her earlier book *The Childhood of Art*, as *its* subtitle emphasizes, is ultimately "an interpretation of Freud's aesthetics," even if its reception so far has been as the first in Kofman's series of books about Freud rather than as the first in her series of writings on aesthetics. As the title of "The Melancholy of Art" implies, it is an essay at the interface of psychoanalysis and aesthetics above all, and Kofman mobilizes various Freudian categories and concepts in the course of her analysis, yet she retains throughout what one might characterize as a deconstructive suspicion of aesthetic "master concepts" (Freudian or other), and her argument reaches a crucial turning point when she makes what is for her (as she establishes elsewhere, notably in her studies of E. T. A. Hoffmann) the characteristically Nietzschean move of breaking off in a peal of laughter (see Large 1999). In such ways she manages successfully in this piece, it seems to me, to play the paternal perspectives off against each other (and by no means just these, either, as we shall see) so that, as my subtitle has it, one can truly speak of "Sarah Kofman's aesthetics" in the fullest sense, the sense of Bloom's "strong interpretation."[4] "La mélancolie de l'art" may not have been translated into English, but it has been translated into German, as "Die Melancholie der Kunst," and was chosen by Peter Engelmann to represent Kofman's work in a collection that also included essays by Lyotard, Derrida, and Foucault.[5] She herself was proud of it, and I think she was right to be.

Kofman's essay "The Melancholy of Art" begins circumspectly; like many of her works that preceded it—*The Childhood of Art*, *Nietzsche and Metaphor*, her first essay on Derrida, "Un philosophe 'unheimlich'" (1973b) and her first collection of essays on Freud, translated as *Freud and Fiction* (1991)—it begins with a self-reflexive moment of self-questioning, of questioning the very possibility of her own discourse, writing on art *as a philosopher*:

> Écrire sur l'art n'est-ce pas là tâche impossible? Qu'est-ce que l'art *en général*? Peut-on tenir un même discours sur l'art dit "représentatif" et sur l'art "moderne"? Et chacun de ces domaines est-il bien un tout homogène? Peut-on, en outre, parler de façon univoque de la musique, de l'architecture, de la sculpture, de la peinture, de la poésie, du cinéma, de la photographie, etc.? Y a-t-il un type d'art que l'on puisse privilégier et qui puisse servir de modèle, de *paradigme*?
>
> Toutes ces questions reposent sur une assurance première, qu'il y a des œuvres d'*art*, et une classification hiérarchique des arts, ce qui présuppose résolue la question ontologique initiale: *qu'est-ce* que l'art? Question elle-même emplie de présupposés métaphysiques. (1985b, 11)

> [Writing on art—is that not an impossible task? What is art *in general*? Can we maintain the same discourse about what is called "representative" art and

> about "modern" art? And is each of these fields really a homogeneous whole? Moreover, can we speak unequivocally of music, architecture, sculpture, painting, poetry, cinema, photography, etc.? Is there one type of art that we might privilege and that might serve as a model, a *paradigm*?
>
> All these questions are based on a primary certainty, that there are works of *art*, and a hierarchical classification of the arts, which in turn presupposes that the initial ontological question has been resolved: *what is* art? A question that is itself replete with metaphysical presuppositions.]

An opening barrage of questions such as this demonstrates the ease with which any discourse on art can become deliriously entangled in its own metaphysical speculations extraneous to the art object—and from the first, from that first question (*what is* art?) which presupposes its own primacy, the primacy of ontology as first philosophy. Although he is not actually mentioned in this essay, Heidegger seems to me to be indirectly addressed in this opening passage, which can be read almost as a pastiche of the opening of his 1936 lecture series "The Origin of the Work of Art." Kofman's anti-Heideggerianism may be more explicit elsewhere, but from the outset of "The Melancholy of Art" she decisively marks her distance from Heideggerian and post-Heideggerian thinking on art (which includes Derrida's *The Truth in Painting*).[6]

Strictly speaking, then, the answer to Kofman's first question ("Writing on art—is that not an impossible task?") is "yes." Strictly speaking, as she puts it later in the essay, "Un tableau ne *veut rien dire*" (1985b, 22): "A picture *means nothing/wants to say nothing*"). If such were its project, it would indeed be inferior to words and would need to be sublated by language in order to receive a meaning that might be clearly communicated. "Between the figurative order of the picture and the discursive order of language there exists a gap [un écart] that nothing can fill" (22). So the philosopher who wants to write about art is faced with what Lyotard would call an insurmountable differend between two incommensurable symbolic regimes, with what Kofman terms "un écart"—an interval, a space, an aporia. This is indeed an "arresting" opening: to think of writing on art, it seems, is to make a kind of category mistake. And how does one move "beyond aporia"? Two paths are sketched out by Kofman in this essay. The first is classified as the more traditional and the more common:

> tenter de combler cet écart par un discours proliférant qui met le tableau "à la question" comme pour lui arracher violemment un secret qu'il garderait silencieusement et pudiquement en réserve. Discours bavard qui dissimule le tableau plus qu'il ne livre le fin mot de l'énigme et qui semble commandé par l'angoisse que suscite l'inquiétante étrangeté de ces "voix du silence." (24)

> [attempting to fill this gap with a proliferating discourse which "interrogates" the painting as if to wrench from it, violently, a secret which it is keeping silently and modestly in reserve. A garrulous discourse that disguises the picture rather than delivering up the final key to the enigma and that seems to be dictated by the anxiety which the uncanniness of these "voices of silence" provokes.]

Such garrulity is the preserve of the gallery guide and the art critic, who generate their interminable discourses overlaid on the image and smother it with descriptions. But this first type of reading, this "garrulous" reading of the art object is also the preserve par excellence of the metaphysical philosopher and the psychoanalyst, seeking violently to rape the art object (gendered feminine), to wrench from it some secret that it is supposedly holding in.

The metaphysical philosopher, then, begins not by subjecting his own method to self-reflexive scrutiny (as does Kofman at the opening of her essay); instead he subjects the artwork to an interrogating, rapacious glare. For all the professed "disinterestedness" of Kant's preferred mode of aesthetic contemplation, then, for all the "respectful distance" that Hegel seeks to maintain from the art object, granting its aesthetic autonomy and its independence from the lascivious, appetitive glance, at the same time his dialectical discourse seeks to consume it without residue, without reserve. Within the structure of Hegel's *Aesthetics*, art is always destined to be sublated by religion, both being moments in the unfolding dialectic of alienated Spirit. In the grand scheme of things, art in general is reduced to a position of subservience, and within the logocentric hierarchy of the arts the visual arts are deemed inferior to the art of poetry, the more adequate expression of Spirit.

What is it about art, Kofman wonders, that prompts such a garrulous exertion of mastery destined to subordinate it and efface its specificity? Why such an expense of libidinal investment? What is at stake? Hegel's "respect" for the work of art can be likened to Diderot's "admiration" for the skill of the portrait painter La Tour in producing such uncanny likenesses of his sitters (an example Kofman gives in her essay "The Resemblance of Portraits") (1984b), or the "respect for women" that she analyzes in Kant and Rousseau (1982)—so many apotropaic defense mechanisms designed to protect against the unsettling potential of their objects. Already at the outset of her essay "The Melancholy of Art," immediately after the barrage of metaphysical questions quoted above, Kofman counters:

> Je voudrais simplement montrer ici que la "question de l'art" est peut-être ce qui contraint à faire bouger ce type d'interrogation, à défaire ce notion de modèle, de paradigme, et qu'elle force à *solliciter* de façon plus générale tout le système des oppositions métaphysiques sur lequel repose classiquement le discours philosophique sur l'art. (1985b, 11–12)

> [I should like simply to show here that the "question of art" is perhaps what requires us to displace this type of [metaphysical] interrogation, to dismantle the notions of model or paradigm, and that it forces us to *appeal* in a more general way to the whole system of metaphysical oppositions on which, classically, the philosophical discourse about art rests.]

So "the question of art," for Kofman, performs a similar function to, say, "the question of style" for Derrida in his analysis of the figure of woman in Nietzsche's texts (the original title of the essay that was to become *Spurs* [see Derrida 1973]), and indeed a similar function to "the question of woman" addressed by Kofman herself in *The Enigma of Woman* (1985a), published in the same year as "The Melancholy of Art." The question of art resists the interrogation of the metaphysical master—the art object is destined to remain enigmatic and, furthermore, uncanny, in the specific sense of Freud's analysis of the term in his 1919 essay "Das Unheimliche," which from Kofman's earliest productions is a recurrent point of reference. Why does Hegel seek to mask the art object, Kofman asks,

> si ce n'est parce que l'art inquiète étrangement "l'Esprit," le dérange, tel un revenant, un fantôme *unheimlich* qui ne se laisserait enchaîner dans la demeure familiale (*heimlich*), trop familiale de l'Esprit? Pourquoi si ce n'est parce qu'avec l'art il y va d'un "reste" non relevable? (1985b, 15)
>
> [if not because "Spirit" finds art uncanny, because art disturbs it like a ghost, an *unheimlich* phantom that will not let itself be chained up in the homely (*heimlich*), all-too-homely dwelling-place of Spirit? Why, if not because art has to do with an unsublatable "residue"?]

At least since Plato, then, the aim of philosophy and of the discursive order in general has been to "subordinate art to the logos and to truth" (Kofman 1985b, 12), to treat the image as a pre-text, a spur to its own speculative elaborations, and to protect itself against the unsettling uncanniness of the art object, which nevertheless retains an irreducible, unsublatable, spectral specificity as simulacrum. (The metaphor of spectrality, we should note, was not born with Derrida's *Specters of Marx*.) The repressed art object (and Kofman is writing here specifically of figurative, mimetic art) will always return to haunt the life that it doubles. Still life, *nature morte*, dead nature: art is the supreme sacrifice of life—in Bataille's sense of a sacrifice that "alters and destroys the victim, kills him but does not neglect him" (Kofman 1985b, 16):

> Pas de double sans dévoration, sans *entame* de ce qui, sans lui, aurait pu passer pour une présence pleine, autosuffisante: le double fait *différer* l'origi-

nal de lui-même, le dé-figure, sollicite et inquiète ce qui sans lui pourrait s'identifier de façon simple, se nommer, se classer dans telle ou telle catégorie déterminée. (1985b, 17–18)

[There is no double without a devouring, without an *encroachment* on what might otherwise have been able to pass for a full and self-sufficient presence: the double makes the original *differ* from itself, dis-figures it, appeals to and troubles what could otherwise easily be identified, named, and classified in such or such a determinate category.]

The uncanny work of art exerts an ambivalent fascination on the viewer—the fascination of the cadaver. This is a point to which Kofman returns in her late discussion of Rembrandt's *Anatomy Lesson*, where she focuses on the open book at the feet of the partially dissected corpse, the text incorporated into the image, which serves to deflect the gaze—the gaze of the anatomy students, our gaze—away from the all-too-gruesome exhibition of mortality toward the splendid allure of the logos, which itself, in turn, embodies the scientific *technē* of the master over the splayed/displayed corpse.

In this case, at least, the question of art is a question concerning technics, but a question also that concerns—troubles, distresses, addresses (*sollicite*)—philosophy, psychoanalysis, and any other regimes of would-be techno-scientific instrumental rationality. For beauty, Kofman speculates, can never be divorced from melancholy: beauty is in mourning for philosophy, she writes ("la beauté [. . .] est comme en deuil de philosophie" [1985b, 20]). Just at the point in "The Melancholy of Art" where Kofman has elaborated the cadaverous connotations of the spectral simulacrum that is the uncanny art object, and argued that the "mirror" of speculative textuality serves as an apotropaic defense mechanism to shield philosophy from the mortifying or maddening potential of the Medusa-like image, she introduces the most speculative argument in the whole essay—yet one that is clearly pivotal, since from it the title of the essay derives. The move is not unexpected if one is familiar with the section of *The Childhood of Art* entitled "The Work of the Death Drives," in which Kofman derives from Freud the observation that "the work of art is more in the service of the death drives than of Eros" (Kofman 1988b, 128).[7] Moreover the cover of the collection *Mélancolie de l'art* further prepares the way by presenting us with an unsettling image of death and the maiden, simply entitled *Arrangement*, by the contemporary French artist Alain Lestié—the beauty of the naked young woman compromised by her pose as a Venus de Milo *de nos jours*, her arms mere severed (bloodred) stumps, in double jeopardy from the shrouded figure of Death hovering in the wings and from the shadowy male who seems to be observing her, equally unseen, from behind.

As an emblematic illustration of this point within the essay "The Melancholy of Art" itself, Kofman cites Diderot's analysis, in his *Salon de 1765*, of a sentimental genre painting by Jean-Baptiste Greuze, *La jeune fille qui pleure son oiseau mort* (*The Young Girl Crying over Her Dead Bird*). In his commentary on this painting, Diderot indulges in an extended speculation on the prehistory of this image, elaborating a bourgeois morality tale, as Kofman points out, according to which scenario the young girl is in fact a lover contemplating the loss of her virginity figured metonymically in the dead canary construed as a gift from her beloved, fatally neglected while she was in the throes of "forgetting herself." Comparing this painting to Greuze's earlier, similar *Le miroir cassé* (*The Broken Mirror*), Diderot protests to his anonymous but evidently naively literalistic interlocutor:

> Ne pensez-vous pas qu'il y aurait autant de bêtise à attribuer les pleurs de la jeune fille de ce Salon à la perte d'un oiseau, que la mélancolie de la jeune fille du Salon précédent à son miroir cassé? Cette enfant pleure autre chose, vous dis-je. (1959, 536)
>
> [Don't you think that it would be as stupid to attribute the tears of the young girl in this Salon to the loss of a bird as it would be to attribute the melancholy of the young girl in the previous Salon to her broken mirror? This child is crying over something else, I tell you.]

Kofman's gloss on this passage itself deserves to be read symptomatically, I would argue, for she herself now indulges in a bout of speculation on her own part as to what this "something else" might be:

> [L]'oiseau est toujours déjà envolé, le miroir cassé, fêlé, et c'est cette brisure du sens que pleure la jeune fille, la perte, avec le miroir et l'oiseau, de toute référence, et donc de tout discours; elle pleure le "sacrifice" du sujet ou la perte de l'objet, ce qui, en effet, selon Freud, engendre la mélancolie jusqu'à ce que s'accomplisse le travail du deuil. (1985b, 21–22)
>
> [The bird has always already flown, the mirror is always already broken, cracked, and it is this shattering of sense that the young girl is crying over, the loss, along with the mirror and the bird, of all reference, and hence of all discourse; she is crying over the "sacrifice" of the subject or the loss of the object, which indeed, according to Freud, produces melancholy until the work of mourning is accomplished.]

At this point, though, Kofman knows that she has pushed her point too far—that *she* is at risk of forgetting herself—and at this juncture she breaks off abruptly, mimicking Diderot's dialogism by herself introducing the questioning voice of an anonymous interlocutor: "But isn't that just another meaning that you are giving to the picture?" (22). By such a self-deconstructive strategy she seeks to preempt any critique of her own discourse, but of course if we do apply the terms of Kofman's analysis of the coercive relation between the figurative and the discursive we know that such an apotropaic gesture is bound to be ineffectual—a point to which I will return shortly in my conclusion.

This abrupt hiatus which marks, in Philippe Lacoue-Labarthe's terms, the caesura of the speculative (see Lacoue-Labarthe 1978), is a decisive moment in the development of Kofman's argument, for it opens up the second type of response to the aporetic impasse that is the incommensurability of the figurative and discursive orders, signaled in Diderot's text by the peal of laughter that rings out in response to the madness of the philosopher's deliriously ingenious overinterpretation.

> Mais, mon ami, ne riez-vous pas, vous, d'entendre un grave personnage s'amuser à consoler un enfant en peinture de la perte de son oiseau, de la perte de tout ce qu'il vous plaira? (Diderot 1959, 536)

> But, my friend, don't you laugh at hearing a serious person amuse himself by consoling a child in a painting over the loss of her bird, over the loss of what you will?

Kofman likens this laughter to the shameless laughter of the Thracian servant-girl reported in an anecdote in Plato's *Theaetetus*, when the distracted philosopher Thales falls into a well. In the context of Kofman's earlier studies we might also assimilate it to the laughter Baubô provokes in Demeter (see Kofman 1979, 263–304), to the Dionysian laughter of the character Belcampo/ Schönfeld in E.T.A. Hoffmann's *The Devil's Elixirs* (see Large 1999), and of Nietzsche's laughing god Dionysus himself. Such laughter, for Kofman, cuts through all the swathes of logocentric discourse and opens up the "space of the caesura" (the title of another of the essays collected in *Mélancolie de l'art*) as the space of indeterminacy, madness, and play, precisely the space that will be occupied and exploited by the nonmimetic abstract art of modernity distinguished by its *éloquence étranglée* (stifled eloquence).[8] This is the title of the last section of Kofman's essay, in which she celebrates Kandinsky's break with figuration, Magritte's play with captions, and Bacon's subversive series art that breaks (with) the structures of totemic, oedipal identification typical of representative art and desacralizes the art object (Benjamin's essay "The Work of Art in the Age of Its Mechanical Reproducibility" [1968] is hovering in the background here). Such examples of modern art, Kofman concludes, throw a new light, *après-coup*, on the figurative painting of the past and serve only to underline the status of the representative art object as the "originary double" of "reality."

And yet, I would argue, this celebratory conclusion to Kofman's essay is itself haunted by a spectral double—by the melancholy of art, the *concept* of the melancholy of art. For if we subject this concept to scrutiny, we should surely ask why it is that beauty should mourn philosophy. Is it not rather the other way around? Is Kofman's construction of the melancholy of art not itself symptomatic of philosophy mourning the loss of its own mastery over art by projecting *its* melancholy onto the art object in a calculated gesture of narcissistic displacement? Is Kofman's own account, in other words, not (inevitably) haunted by the repressed, "garrulous" kind of reading?

Kofman's essay begins: "I should like simply to show here that the 'question of art' is perhaps what requires us to displace this type of [metaphysical] interrogation." But such a desire must face up to the ("structural") impossibility of its fulfillment, for just as "a painting means nothing," and by the same token no text can "simply show" anything. Kofman's text, ultimately, is denied that access to—that translation into—the iconic that it so desires. Just as Nietzsche writes in the *nachträglich* 1886 preface to *The Birth of Tragedy* that "it should have *sung*, this 'new soul'—rather than spoken!" (2000, 6), so one might say of Kofman's endeavor: it should have been *painted*, this new aesthetic.

"The question of art" docs not have any definitive, univocal answer—such as, for example, "the melancholy of art." "The question of art" is a question addressed to philosophy, more akin (on Kofman's account, at least) to the disruptive *operations* that are deconstruction and psychoanalysis in that, by agonally confronting philosophy with an aporia, it obliges philosophy, in fact, to speculate on itself and its own constraints. Kofman brings to bear on aesthetic questions, and the question of aesthetics in general, the practiced eye of the (psycho)genealogist for whom (to speak with Nietzsche) philosophical aesthetics is but a semiotics and a symptomatology, and whose disruptive diagnoses seek to excavate and expose the turbulent Dionysian *(Ab)Grund* that the apparent serenity of any Apollonian exterior always imperfectly dissimulates. Kofman's essay "The Melancholy of Art" outlines magnificently, meticulously, and exuberantly the contours and implications of the question with which it opens and on which it dwells, but ultimately the mute art object-subject will always, for Kofman, have the last laugh, and *generate* the last laugh on the part of any philosopher who appropriately recognizes the impossibility of his or her enterprise.

Notes

Translations of Kofman's texts are the author's, unless indicated otherwise.

1. See, for example, Sarah Kofman, *Rousseau und die Frauen*, trans. Ruthard Stäblein (Tübingen: Rive Gauche, 1985).

2. Sarah Kofman, "La mélancolie de l'art," in *Philosopher: Les interrogations contemporaines. Matériaux pour un enseignement*, ed. Christian Delacampagne and Robert Maggiori (Paris: Fayard, 1980), 415–27; revised republication in Kofman 1985b, 9–33.

3. See Deleuze's own classification of his work on the inside cover of *Dialogues* (Paris: Flammarion, 1977).

4. Kofman comments on her method: "As for Freud and for Nietzsche (on whom I have worked most constantly), these are my two 'great' thinkers: both of them have left a profound impression on me, and they have given me the most, from a philosophical and psychological point of view. But they are not masters. I prevent Freud from gaining mastery through Nietzsche, and I prevent Nietzsche from gaining mastery through Freud. I deconstruct the one with the other" (1993a, 12).

5. Sarah Kofman, "Die Melancholie der Kunst," in *Postmoderne und Dekonstruktion: Texte französischer Philosophen der Gegenwart*, ed. Peter Engelmann (Stuttgart: Reclam, 1990), 224–43.

6. See especially Kofman 1983a, where Heidegger's Plato is taken to task, and the introduction to Kofman 1992, 11–43, translated by Duncan Large in "Explosion I: Of Nietzsche's *Ecce Homo*," *Diacritics* 24, no. 4 (Winter 1994): 51–70, in which Kofman takes issue with Heidegger's reading of a passage from Nietzsche's *The Gay Science*, characterizing it as, ultimately, Christian and thus misplaced. See also Derrida 1978.

7. Kofman 1970, 188: "[L]'œuvre d'art est plus au service des pulsions de mort que d'Éros." For the link between beauty, mourning, and the uncanny, see also Kofman 1995a, 9–48, translated by Duncan Large in Deutscher and Oliver 1999, 25–48.

8. See also Kofman 1987c.

CHAPTER 2

Sarah Kofman's Art of Affirmation, or the "Non-illusory Life of an Illusion"

PLESHETTE DeARMITT

> Art and laughter, when they go together, do not run counter to suffering, they do not ransom or redeem it, but live off it; as for salvation, redemption, and resurrection, the absence of any illusion shines like a ray of living light through all of Sarah's work.
>
> —Jacques Derrida

In the eponymously titled chapter of her final book, *L'imposture de la beauté*, posthumously published in 1995,[1] Kofman turns her attention to Oscar Wilde's modern rewriting of the Narcissus myth in *The Picture of Dorian Gray* and takes up the themes of art and doubles, beauty and ruin, life and death, as well as mourning and melancholy. In "The Imposture of Beauty," Kofman recalls the lessons taught by Freud in a very slight piece entitled "On Transience" ("Vergänglichkeit"). There, he recounts a summer stroll in the countryside, taken with "a taciturn friend" and a young, but accomplished, poet. To Freud's surprise, each companion is unable to take pleasure in the beauty of the nature around him, because each has already begun to lament the fact that not only the particular beauty on this summer day but also that all beauty found in nature and art is destined to decay and perish. Freud concludes that the necessary decline of all that is perfect and beautiful "gives rise to two different impulses in the mind": on the one hand, "despondency" over the potential loss of beauty and, on the other, "rebellion" against the fact of this inevitable loss (1916, 305). Beauty, even in full flowering, foreshadows its own demise, causing, what Freud describes as, "a foretaste of mourning" (306). The idea that beauty is not immortal, but merely transient, causes both despondency or "a foretaste of mourning" and rebellion or revolt against mourning, in other words, both mourning and the refusal of mourning. Freud tries to demonstrate to his walking companions that the worth of all that is beautiful only increases, rather than decreasing, due to its transience, due to its "scarcity value in time" (307). Although unsuccessful in his attempt to persuade his companions, Freud perseveres in his effort to convince his readers that one must mourn the evanescence of beauty and, thus, affirm it in all its fragility.

Despite the brevity of Freud's essay, a mere three pages long, Kofman finds there issues of the utmost concern: the desire for immortality, the ambivalent nature of beauty, mourning and melancholy, and affirmation in spite of loss. I would like to suggest that Sarah Kofman, in her own terms, rewrote Freud's "On Transience" in an even more condensed and cryptic formulation. We find her re-inscription of this essay on the back cover of her 1985 text, *Mélancolie de l'art*. Below, I reproduce this passage, after which I will work out its logic, line by line.

> Et si la beauté qui camoufle le caractère évanescent de toute chose était elle-même éphémère? Le déclin de ce qui rend tolérable l'intolérable susciterait vertige et désarroi.
>
> Ce refus du deuil de la beauté est révélateur de la fonction cathartique de l'art aussi mystifiante que celle du spéculatif, miroir captateur d'images par trop bouleversantes, insupportables.
>
> Briser avec ce qui dans l'art répond à notre demand d'éternité c'est disloquer l'espace de la representation et du sens, c'est inventer un espace d'indétermination et de jeu—ouvrir un tout autre espace.
>
> Aussi la beauté n'est-elle jamais exempte de mélancholie. . . .
>
> [And what if the beauty that conceals the evanescent nature of all things were itself ephemeral? The decline of what renders the intolerable tolerable would cause vertigo and disarray.
>
> This refusal of the mourning of beauty reveals the cathartic function of art, which is as mystifying as the speculative, a mirror capturing images that are too overwhelming, unbearable.
>
> To break with everything in art that responds to our desire for eternity is to dislocate the space of representation and meaning; it is to invent a space of indetermination and play—to open up a wholly other space.
>
> Beauty is never exempt from melancholy. . . .]

I. The Mask of Beauty, or the Illusion of Immortality

And what if the beauty that hides the evanescent aspect of all things were itself ephemeral?

At least since Plato, beauty has served a salutary function—that of protecting mortals from all that is contingent—by granting them access to that which is eternal and incorruptible. As we recall from both the *Symposium* and *Phaedrus*, beauty not only shines eternally, but also, by virtue of its radiance, awakens in those captivated by it a recollection of all that is eternal. Through the face of the beloved, always a fair and unblemished youth, beauty emanates, flooding the lover's soul and awakening his memory of the true and the good. As Socrates says at *Greater Hippias* 279b, "it looks as though beauty is metaphorically a kind of father of the good" (Plato 1961, 1551). Thus, beauty has provided mortals with the reassuring face of eternity.

Before we can explore Kofman's demystification of beauty, of which Derrida says she "cruelly lays bare a cathartic function, the sublimation at work in art or in the experience of beauty" (Derrida 1997, 142), we must examine the nature of beauty and the desire for it.[2] In "The Imposture of Beauty," Kofman exposes the artist's, in this case Basil Hallward's, fascination with ideal beauty—a beauty that escapes all decline and ruin, a beauty that is eternally luminous. For Basil, Dorian Gray, his model and muse, possesses "the secret wonder he is seeking . . . of which the visible beauty of Dorian is just a shadow or a mere pattern" (Wilde 1992, 36). Kofman claims that "this wonder is ideal beauty, the idea of beauty such as might be contemplated by the initiate in Plato's *Symposium*, who is sent into unimaginable raptures at the end of the dialectic: an unchanging, eternal, marmoreal beauty that nothing can taint, wither, or ravage and that, in contrast to physical beauty, is not destined to decay" (1995a, 27).

Ideal beauty or the idea of beauty is often embodied in the delicate figure of a flower. Wilde's text, which is, above all, a meditation on the nature of art and beauty, is filled with "an abundance of flowers, whose dazzling beauty and verticality," Kofman writes, "mask their fragility and transience, making one forget their foul-smelling origins" (33). Kofman declares that this exemplary image and symbol of beauty, from Ovid's narcissus to Kant's tulip, is an imposture—"an imposture of beauty because, by its very splendor, it appears to protect us from the loss of our narcissistic securities, from any fall, any flaw, failure, defilement, degradation, corruption—from ruin, the defeat with which, in reality, beauty itself is fatally threatened" (33).

This privileged symbol of beauty, which is often erected in the place of a loss, particularly a death, restores our faith in the immortality of beauty or, more accurately, in beauty as immortality. This "imposture of beauty," of which Kofman speaks, can be seen in Ovid's version of the Narcissus myth. In the *Metamorphoses*, Ovid so thoroughly takes Narcissus to task for being entranced, for being endlessly fascinated with the beautiful image before him and, without mercy, depicts the tragic fate of Narcissus. Due to Narcissus's refusal to turn away from an impossible desire—one that denies any loss, separation, or division, he is doomed to perish. Even though Ovid's Narcissus is punished for his morbid fascination with his double, Ovid offers his reader a captivating double—a replacement for the corpse of Narcissus—as a figure of consolation. I will cite Ovid's conclusion: Narcissus "sat his tired head to rest on the grass. And then dark death shut fast his eyes that had been captured by the beauty of their master. . . . His Naiad sisters, in lament, as an offering for their brother, cropped their hair. The Dryads also wept. The choir of grief was joined by Echo as she mimed their sounds. They had prepared the pyre, the bier, the torches; but nowhere could they find Narcissus' body: where it had been, they found instead a flower, its yellow center circled by white petals" (1993, 97).

Narcissus is double—both lover and beloved, both flesh and image, both mortal and immortal, both corpse and flower. Narcissus as flower averts the reader's "gaze" away from Narcissus the corpse, and thus shields him or her from directly facing what Kofman terms "the intolerable." Furthermore, the flower is also double, as it is both "a symbol of the evanescence of human beauty *and* its imposture, for all that it makes us believe in the illusion of its eternity and serves as an 'Apollonian' mask, a screen protecting us from the intolerable 'Dionysian' reality" (Kofman 33; emphasis mine). Beauty's power, according to Kofman, is not only to captivate and entrance, but also to ward off all that is utterly unbearable—"the intolerable."

II. An Economy of the Intolerable and Tolerable

> *The decline of what makes the intolerable tolerable would cause vertigo and disarray.*

In order to understand this passage in particular and to elaborate Kofman's aesthetics in general, we must first make sense of a pivotal phrase found all over her corpus, what Derrida refers to as "an economical formulation" and, even more strongly, as a "formulation of economy itself" (Derrida 1997, 142). This phrase—"rendre tolérable l'intolérable" ["to render or make the intolerable tolerable"]—reveals not just an economy, but also a logic, a logic that frustrates the logic of noncontradiction, not to mention her readers. In order to elaborate this logic and economy, we must find, in Kofman's texts, figures of the tolerable and intolerable—for example, the mask of beauty, the head of Medusa, and the image of the cadaver.

But, if one could claim that there are two figures that exemplify the economy and logic of the tolerable and intolerable, they would be Nietzsche's Apollo and Dionysus. In her 1979 text *Nietzsche et la scène philosophique*, Kofman reinterprets these paradigmatic Nietzschean figures not as deities, but as doubles "that do not oppose each other like two concepts, but as two forces that are destined to conjure [*conjurer*] one another" (1979, 67). One must hear her use of "conjurer" in its double resonance: to conjure away or ward off *and* to conjure up or call forward. Thus, Apollo and Dionysus, on Kofman's reading, are interminably embroiled in a conjuring game.

Kofman argues that Dionysus, who is too unbearable to behold, never shows himself as himself, but only appears under various names, wearing different masks. Therefore, he must show up on the scene in the guise of another, for example, in the image of Apollo. Yet this is no mere example, because Apollo is image itself. Hence Apollo's luminous visage is not simply his own, but it is also the mask of Dionysus. Likewise, for Dionysus to "reveal" himself as Apollo, he cannot be pure presence or the voice of truth. Instead, Kofman claims, Dionysus is "always already divided, split, always already Apollinian" (1979, 72).

The beautiful face of Apollo, then, functions as the mask of Dionysus, "in the double sense of the term . . . [as the] face and manifestation of him, but also the veil over him" (59). Despite Kofman's insistence that the appearing of Apollo both reveals and conceals Dionysus, she admits that his brilliant image dissimulates "to the point of bringing about a 'forgetting' of the one of whom he is the double" (59). It is precisely "this moment of radical 'forgetting' of the Dionysian . . . [that] provokes the 'metaphysical' trap of an essential opposition between Apollo and Dionysus, surface and depth, philosophy and art, knowledge and life" (60). According to the Nietzsche of *The Birth of Tragedy*, "Greek art taught us that there is no truly beautiful surface without a terrifying depth" (Kofman 1979, 58). This surface is neither a transparent mirror, nor a simple reflection, but a mask whose function is to veil a "fearsome depth" (58). It is Nietzsche who showed Kofman that only the Apollinian image, which is by its nature beautiful, can render the intolerable—death, suffering, the ambiguities of becoming, in a word, the Dionysian—tolerable (Kofman 1985b, 75).

III. Catharsis, or an Impossible Mourning

> *This refusal of the mourning of beauty reveals the cathartic function of art, which is as mystifying as the speculative, a mirror catching images that are too overwhelming, unbearable. . . . Beauty is never exempt from melancholy.*

Another figure that Kofman deploys in many of her texts, including *Camera Obscura and Mélancolie de l'art*, is that of Medusa. Like Dionysus, Medusa destroys those who dare to cast their gaze upon her. This intolerable creature causes those who are fascinated by her to become petrified like a corpse. How then does one prevail over this death-bearing Gorgon? Perseus found a way to protect himself from Medusa and to gain an advantage over her, so that he could bring her head home. Using his polished breastplate as a mirror, he turned Medusa against herself "by terrifying her, by petrifying [*medusé*] her with the look of her own image, with her double" (1979, 68). Kofman writes that only "the artistic figure of Medusa is capable of triumphing over the horrible Medusa, stripped [*dépouillé*] of all veils" (1985b, 75). Perseus could, however, only triumph over Medusa because she is also double—both fascinating and fascinated, petrifying and petrified, naked and veiled, horrible and beautiful. Perseus could only transform this unbearable figure into a work of art, because she too is already Apollinian—already the bearer of an image.

Yet, what concerns us is the cathartic function of the image. From her first to her last book, Kofman repeatedly insists upon the pharmaceutical power of art—"the sublimation at work in art or in the experience of beauty" (Derrida 1997, 142). Inherent in the nature of the artistic image is a certain power of occultation or mystification, which Kofman affirms as therapeutic. The ruse of Apollo is that he "create[s] pleasant illusions and powerful mirages in order to destroy the Titans, to overcome the monsters, to triumph over the terrifying depth by petrifying [*medusé*] it" (Kofman 1979, 68). The Apollinian power of the image is precisely its apotropaic effect, which Kofman describes as "the inverse of looking into the sun" (70). In the case of looking directly into the sun, one's sight is protected by the production of dark spots. Conversely, when one looks into "the horrible Night," into an intolerable darkness, one's vision is cured by blinding light (70–71).

Apollo's blinding beauty brings about a "forgetting," a forgetting of his double, Dionysus. This "forgetting" of the Dionysian, or in psychoanalytic language this "repression" of the intolerable, appears to be originary, even necessary. Is Kofman then endorsing a "forgetting" or "repression" that buys into the dream of redemption and salvation? Is that not art and beauty's great power—to ward off death and thus to deny the need for mourning? Is she arguing that the function of art is to create an illusion of "blessed security," by transforming an intolerable "reality" into a tolerable "illusion"? Or is she, like the Freud of *The Future of an Illusion*, asking us to abandon all illusions, to grow up, and to refuse to be childishly and narcissistically enchanted by art and beauty? Is she instructing us to forsake that which makes life bearable, to tear the veils and masks off of the unbearable, and to look directly and indecently at that which should not be seen? I would like to suggest that in her writings on art Kofman does not decide between these two responses to art and beauty. For Kofman, to cling pathologically to beauty's Apollinian mask with all its promises of immortality or to believe naively that Dionysus, let alone we mere mortals, can exist without the veil of beauty is to misunderstand the double nature of art and images, which requires a double reading and a double affirmation. Kofman's double affirmation of art says "yes" to the melancholy of, or the impossibility of, mourning beauty and "yes" to the necessity of mourning the eternity of beauty.

IV. The Art of Amor Fati

> *To break with everything in art that responds to our desire for eternity is to dislocate the space of representation and meaning; it is to invent a space of indetermination and play—to open up a wholly other space.*

In an untitled homage for Sarah Kofman, published in abridged form in *The Work of Mourning*, Derrida grapples with the loss of his friend of over twenty years and with how to receive and care for the corpus she left behind. In his work of mourning, Derrida tries to bear witness to Kofman's art of life, which necessarily includes a thinking of death that is inscribed, as he says, "in Sarah's great book in so many volumes" (Derrida 1997, 142). In response to her call that art ought to break with its desire for eternity, Derrida declares that "this is . . . the most important point, the most difficult argument—the consequence that Sarah Kofman draws from this double mystification is not the injunction to get over mourning this impossible mourning, not to abandon art, beauty or the speculative. Quite the contrary. In breaking with the 'desire for eternity' that engenders at once mourning and the impossibility of mourning, mourning and melancholy, *it is necessary* [*il faut*]—and here is the injunction or, at least, the necessity, in its most enigmatic, most fatalistic, sense of this term—it is necessary 'to invent' [*il faut 'inventer'*]" (143).

Let us look more carefully at this spare and singular imperative that Sarah Kofman leaves us with. If the "*it is necessary*" [*il faut*], as Derrida suggests, should be read as double: indicating both "lack or mourning and joyous necessity," then Kofman's prescription for art would entail both mourning and a refusal of mourning (Derrida 1997, 143). In her relentless demystification of art and beauty's claim to immortality, she insists upon a work of mourning, a mourning for "the eternity of beauty." In "The Imposture of Beauty," Kofman analyzes Dorian Gray's fetishizing of beauty, which she links to his inability to mourn its ephemeral nature. Dorian, like Freud's young poet friend, "for whom the fragility and evanescence of beauty seem necessarily to devalue it and to give rise to a feeling of disgust at the fleetingness of this world," is incapable of affirming beauty or art and, hence, unable to affirm life (Kofman 1995a, 41). The revolt against mourning the transience of beauty is, for Kofman, none other than a "refusal of death," which is both a fear of death and life (1988a, 128). A Kofmanian affirmation of art and beauty "is nothing other than a certain thought of death [that is] neither opposition nor indifference to death" (Derrida 1997, 138). This affirmation mourns that beauty with all its masks, cannot protect, redeem or resurrect us, as it is itself fatally flawed. Thus, this affirmative mourning is all too aware that art and beauty cannot offer salvation "from pain, anxiety, illness—and death." Although art promises "neither resurrection nor redemption," it nonetheless remains for Kofman "a necessity to which we must yield" (Derrida 1997, 136–137).

Yet, as Kofman claims, beauty is itself incapable of mourning and hence "is never exempt from melancholy." Inherent in the nature of beauty and the work of art is the work of repression—a repression of all that troubles or threatens its independence and immortality. Art, in Kofman's estimation, always appears to be victorious over all intolerable contingencies, which nevertheless continue to haunt it. Likewise, in the language of Nietzsche, the Apollinian brings about a "forgetting" of the Dionysian, on which it is dependant. This "repression" or "forgetting," which resists the work of mourning, is nonetheless "art's work" (Derrida 1997, 151). Therefore, art and beauty bear the burden of melancholy—at once resistant to mourning and unable to cease mourning. The "melancholy of art or beauty" is "an inability to get over or to be done with mourning, the very failure of mourning that it nonetheless endures" (21). Beauty's melancholy can be witnessed in the symmetry and grace of Greek statues, as well as in the flawless face of Dorian Gray. As Kofman says, a "profound sadness" inhabits their perfect and luminous forms. Indeed, Apollo's light always casts Dionysus's shadow.

Art and beauty, through "illusion," engage us in the ruse of repression and hence "remain in the service of occultation" (Derrida 1997, 151). How is it that Kofman can accept and affirm what she has so consistently and rigorously worked to demystify? She does not give up on light or illusion, which are so essential to art and beauty, because, like Nietzsche, she wrests them from their service to "the True and the Good" (Kofman 1979, 71). Kofman describes Nietzsche's revaluation of the sun and all that is associated with it: "[W]hat is new here is, in relation to Plato and the other Greek myths where light and the sun are agents of salvation, it is only for Nietzsche that light and the sun do not gain their pharmaceutical power from the True and the Good . . . but from appearance and illusion, from blindness. Here, it is a matter of 'another version of the sun'" (71).

Kofman does not negate the illusion of art and beauty, but affirms another light, which still possesses pharmaceutical powers and provides serenity without salvation. As Derrida so eloquently explains: "[S]he does so in order to both have some fun with [art] and to subscribe to it, to laugh at it but also to approve of, love, affirm, and repeat it, the affirmation of art . . . even in its function of occultation or illusion, the *non-illusory life of an illusion*, manifesting, affirming and still holding on to life, carrying it living right to its limit" (Derrida 1997, 151, emphasis mine). Even repression, he argues, would for Kofman, "be yet another ruse of affirmation, a *trop* and a trope, an excess and a figure of the 'yes' to life, a number or figure of the *amor fati*" (141).

While she does not abandon art or beauty, which she has cast in different light, Sarah Kofman insists that "*it is necessary to invent.*" But, what should be invented under the name of art? Although her answer is playful and not programmatic, it is urgent and resolute nonetheless—what should, what ought, what must be invented is "a space of indetermination and play," "a wholly other space." I will conclude this chapter, as Kofman closed so many of her written works, by giving the last word to another through citation. I will once again call upon Derrida's reading of his colleague's remarkable corpus. Of this wholly other space, where indetermination and play reign, he writes, it "would not be deserted by the beautiful; it would not be a desert of art and beauty. It would open the way to another affirmation, other but older, more ancient; and since it too remains to come, this affirmation is also younger than everything it endures, through, and thus beyond, if this is possible, the experience of an impossible mourning become possible" (Derrida 1997, 143).

Notes

Unless otherwise noted, the translations of Koman's texts are the author's own.

1. Sarah Kofman, "L'imposture de la beauté: l'inquiétante étrangeté du *Portrait de Dorian Gray*, d'Oscar Wilde" in Kofman 1995a [9–48]. English version: "The Imposture of Beauty: The Uncanniness of Oscar Wilde's *The Picture of Dorian Gray*," trans. Duncan Large, in Deutscher and Oliver 1999 [25–48].

2. All page references made to Derrida 1997 will be to the French version of his untitled homage for Sarah Kofman. I am grateful to Pascale-Anne Brault and Michael Naas for kindly permitting me to use their unpublished translation of this essay, which will appear in Sarah Kofman's *Selected Writings* forthcoming with Stanford University Press. An abridged version of this text can be found in Derrida 2001.

CHAPTER 3

Sarah Kofman's Wit

ANN SMOCK

I hope to capture something of Sarah Kofman's high-spirited irreverence in the following—something of her insubordination. If jokes, wordplay, and paradoxes interested and pleased her a great deal, it was in large part because of the prospect they hold out for tripping up the greats of this world: of toppling the adults (that is, those who made you renounce childhood) back over into childhood themselves, and of winding them up in the coils of language that they forbade you to play with when you were small. "To exult in the paralyzing snarls of language," she wrote in *Comment s'en sortir*, "is always also to exult in snaring the grownups and snarling your parents up in a net like the one Hephaistos fashioned to trap Ares and Aphrodite in. That was a spectacle," she adds, "that made all the gods of Olympus laugh (they were all there to catch that primal scene)" (Kofman 1983a, 32).[1]

To defy the masters, to mock the censors, and to find a way past them, refusing to be hemmed in: these impulses, I think, motivated quite a lot of Sarah Kofman's writing. She found herself hemmed in on many fronts, and she was always looking for a way out, a *poros*. She was always inventing and borrowing good expedients, for—this is my hypothesis—she was unwilling to lament her fate, but was also disinclined to be consoled by illusions. She did not believe there was a way out, ultimately. She was unwilling to believe, then, or not believe, I'd say—unwilling to be duped or disillusioned either, and so she played, to use an expression she herself often employs—on two terrains at once: the terrain of confidence and the terrain of despair, uncompromisingly.

In this respect she resembles Eros, the child that Penia, who got left out on the doorstep like a beggar when the gods gathered to feast, cleverly contrived to conceive with Poros as he sleepily luxuriated, drunk on nectar. Eros, Kofman wrote, inherited the contradictory characteristics of both his parents—those of his female parent, Penia the indigent, and those of his male parent, Poros, rich in resources. Eros himself is neither rich nor poor, female nor male, but rather just as apt to let slip through his fingers all the gains his cleverness wins him as he is fertile with clever stratagems whenever hardship grips him. Eros is a daimon, Kofman writes, in *Comment s'en sortir* (Kofman

1983a, 60–61); he is an intermediary being, foreign to the logic of identity and a stranger to simple oppositions. Neither mortal nor immortal, neither a fool nor a sage, he spends all his life philosophizing.

Humorists can do without illusions and still not sink under the weight of life's injustices. Sarah Kofman evokes their capacity for buoyant clearheadedness in *Quatre romans analytiques* (Kofman 1974, 17).[2] Very few people, however, are able to get along without some form of mystification, she observes, with Freud. Only an elite is capable of humor (see 1991, 6). Humor enables one to bear up under duress and do one's part in the serious efforts that civilization demands but not by offering, as Freud sometimes considered that art does, a little recreational space within culture where adults, complacently believing they are in touch with Higher Things, can give in and play, without scruple, like children. Rather, humor shows that even the most daunting tasks an adult is called upon to undertake are not much different from a child's amusements. And it is not everyone who can afford to recognize the frivolity in the profoundest matters, or acknowledge that science, say, and fiction are not strictly opposites.

Not everyone can do without belief in a Truth that, once laid bare, presents itself *en propre*, just as it is. It takes unusual vitality, Kofman says, in her Nietzsche voice, to love illusion for life's sake and consent to be duped; only a few are deep enough to rejoice in masks and delight in surfaces, or beautiful enough to go naked like Dionysos, showing sheer appearance unveiled, dismissing the opposition between truth and illusion and saying that life is neither surface nor depth, concealed nor unconcealed. Few are light enough, fleet or false enough.[3] Freud, indeed, generally approached literature as a seductive outer garment woven out of metaphors, decorated with elaborate textual designs, and concealing underneath the one thing that really matters, a secret, psychoanalytic truth, which he reveals, by removing the fine outer covering, a mere shimmering appearance, and pouncing on the meaning, the one. If he took a keen interest in myths and legends, it was inasmuch as he discerned in them misty versions of science—infantile stammerings barely intelligible until they resonated faintly with his own strictly rigorous and illuminating formulations, at which point, clarified, unified, they fell into line with and corroborated his masterful insights. He arranged thus, Kofman observes, to preserve a belief he could not altogether do without, in reality's independence from appearance, and truth's from fantasy; and he indulged his own fantasy of himself as a dauntless riddle-solver.

Kofman shows that it is not when he's masterfully dissolving imaginary fabrications the better to find the truth that they disguise that he is free of illusions, but rather when he recognizes in the object of his research something that never does present itself unmasked, undisguised, as itself, *en propre*—something like the death drive, which cannot be apprehended directly, but only manifests itself obliquely under a variety of names, in different guises and disguises, and which though it no doubt accounts for oppositions among the various psychic agencies cannot itself be accounted for or explained, unless by recourse to myth. Between science and myth, the irrefutably real and the fictional, there is not always a clear-cut difference. "The doctrine of the instincts is so to speak our mythology," Freud wrote (Kofman quotes him in Kofman 1974, 44; my translation). Elsewhere, however—for example, in the essay he wrote on Hoffmann's *Sandman*—he arranges to gloss over (at least this is Kofman's view) the diabolical force of the death instinct, which divides every presence in two at least, making everything other than itself and inseparable from what is most different from it.[4]

Nevertheless, it is he who writes, in "Humor," that a grownup, well past childish ways and facing reality with resolute lucidity, may easily fall into an uncharacteristic mood that erases the opposition between the real world and the imaginary one. And he may remember, then, the high seriousness with which he used to play at make-believe as a child. And then it may occur to him to compare his current grave occupations with those childish games. That is when he laughs; that is when he "frees himself," Freud says, "from the heavy oppression of life and wins the superior enjoyment of humor."[5]

Whoever can make light thus of his own importance, laughing at the apparent significance of his difficult undertakings in the real so-called world, as well as at the worries that harass him and the dread he feels, sets himself well above any harm that failure or humiliation could do him. From that vantage point nothing that threatens or belittles him appears very important. Granted, the humorist's higher enjoyment seems to come at his own expense: he laughs at his own effortful, embattled self. And indeed it seems that in the humorist the ego shrinks. But the superego grows proportionately, and thanks to its strength, the humorist is able to surpass and make light of his feebleness. For rather than oppress the shrunken little ego cruelly, as in psychosis, this strapping superego kindly deigns to encourage it, saying in effect, "But look! This world that seems to you so dangerous: it's a child's game! So the best idea is to joke and laugh" (Kofman 1983b, 114).

It is this cheerfully imperturbable self-confidence that the humorist shares with the great criminal as described by Nietzsche—the outlaw who thinks of himself only as that which he surpasses and who therefore cannot be touched by anything that is apt to weaken him, such as fright. Beautiful and unreachable women, whom Freud describes in "An Introduction to Narcissism" (describes and then flees, according to Kofman in *L'enigme de la femme*), likewise hold an unattackable position far above their own frailties. Their extreme attractiveness and their strangeness, too, come from their serene autonomy. Freud compares them to humorists on account of this unflappable self-sufficiency. The triumph of humor implies an unassailable narcissism, Kofman writes (1980, 65–66).[6]

And Freud himself triumphs, thanks to humor, she observes—triumphs over the dogged resistance of his most ornery patients: he wins out by suggesting, for example, to one such obstinate patient, as an interpretation of his stubborn silence, that he considered it too expensive to be cured and was unwilling to pay the price of his sessions with the doctor. On that occasion Freud received as his reward a splendid slip from the indignant patient, a real gift: "Money is nothing to me," he exclaimed, and named a sum in shillings by mistake, instead of pounds, that he would not hesitate to spend—which made even him laugh and good-naturedly grant Freud the relevance of his interpretation. For a *lapsus linguae* is often not unlike a comical play on words. And lest Freud's critics, with whom he also has to contend, consider that such an example of a contribution by the patient himself toward the interpretation of his case does not really argue as well as it is meant to against the charge that the analyst never pays any attention to anything a patient says—never even grants to him the right to speak unless it be to confirm the analyst's own views, but shows, quite to the contrary, that the analyst is always lying in wait to catch the patient in a trap—lest his critics face him, then, with this objection and attack him in this manner (suggesting that he is bent on nothing so much as the relentless demonstration of his own mastery and the domination of his patient), Freud emerges triumphant once again, by laughing: by laughing at his own impotence this time, and getting his detractors to laugh along with him. This time he refers to the patient for whom the painfulness of recovering is so much worse than the pain of his illness that he reacts to any hint of progress in the analysis by becoming markedly sicker. So the deterioration of his condition confirms the accuracy of the analyst's construction.

Freud's very failure to cure the sufferer—his very helplessness before the patient's indomitable refusal to see things his way and submit—proves that Freud is right. But it would not serve Freud's purpose, in his argument with his critics, to emphasize this triumph—this proof of his power brought even by his helplessness—and he barely does. He stresses rather the indisputable superiority of the death drive, the ultimate victory of death, the sole master, and of time, the only factor in psychoanalysis that ever decides anything definitively. For not even the best gifts that patients sometimes grant the analyst mean anything conclusive, Freud acknowledges; at most they hint that the analyst's interpretation will be confirmed further along in the treatment. So finally Freud compares himself to the valet in a farce by Nestroy who, whenever he is questioned about anything, always answers, "Everything will become clear in the course of things." By equating his own earnest claims with the comical tag of a valet in a drawing room farce, Freud transforms a tragic, paranoid trial scene, Kofman says, into a laughing matter. Given that time and death alone are masters, humor enables one to avoid despair and rise above one's misfortune by laughing at it. And this victorious laughter implies an unshakable narcissism that faces the worst unperturbed. After all, life is just a game, a farce. It is better to laugh than to weep. A strategy that turns out to be no good, an interpretation that proves wrong, can always be dismantled and reconstructed differently on another day. Freud, Kofman writes, gambles and plays on the farcical stage of psychoanalysis, casting the dice again and again, "dans le risque et le rire."[7]

This unshakable narcissism, though—this happy self-possession, the humorist's impregnable position—implies that there is no such thing. No such perfect self-sufficiency, that is; no such simple, happy mastery that a servile double has not edged aside, as it were, and caused to differ from itself, granting it in this contradictory way alone its carefree self-assurance. For the insouciant gambler maintains his loftiness by stooping to the level of a calculating domestic. He loses and attains his happy position simultaneously. His identity withdraws from him, you might say, and crowns him, both.

So humor muddies up the clear distinction between victory and defeat, mastery and abjection; it shows that gaiety dwells in despair. This is what Sarah Kofman emphasizes in *Conversions*, her study of *The Merchant of Venice*, where she writes that Shakespeare reveals all at once the vanity of human life and the vanity of all simple oppositions.[8] Lodging madness inside wisdom and comedy within tragedy, he shows the interdependence of time's two faces, mania and melancholy (Kofman 1987a, 69). Indeed, that hilarity and desperation are doubles, that triumph and humiliation cannot be disentangled, is what Kofman demonstrates regularly in her work, and she does it with a particularly disarming vehemence, it seems to me, in the essay she called "Le battu imbattable," where comedy is not the slightest bit funny, but utter degradation is unbelievably exhilarating.[9]

In this short piece, she depicts the humorist as a man who, en route to fame as a scientist, ends up famous as a clown instead, and not just famous but absolutely unbeatable. The act he puts on night after night gets more laughs than any other clown act, and in it he receives more beatings than anyone can keep track of. "Performance inégalable," Kofman writes. She stayed up all night once, I gather, writing "Le battu imbattable" after she happened to see a silent movie from the 1920s on television—*He Who Gets Slapped.*

It is the story of a brilliant young man on the verge of a great scientific discovery who is robbed, by the man he considered his benefactor, of his name, his reputation, his research, and his lover. When he presents his work before the Academy of Sciences, the baron, his former protector who has already claimed the same work as his own, slaps him. The assembled academicians drown out his protests with their scoffing laughter when he attempts to defend himself. He retreats weeping to the arms of his beloved, but she too slaps him, in the presence of the baron, her new lover, and laughs at him for thinking that he, no great man after all but a clown, could ever please her.

How can he possibly survive this redoubled slap? Sarah Kofman asks. How can he not feel the world crumble and the earth cease going round?

But it never ceases to go round, she observes. Robbery and betrayal keep it turning ever so smoothly—like a circus ball on a seal's nose. And, indeed, the one who gets nothing in life but slaps makes it go round himself when, acting out his own terrible story evening after evening in his clown suit for the tremendous amusement of a crowd, he spins a big globe as part of his hilarious act. He quits crying, Kofman says, the better to laugh with everyone else at himself, a ludicrous clown, and at the whole world, a clown show.

He manages to turn tragedy into comedy by switching from a passive to an active position with respect to his disgrace, she writes. Of his own accord he assumes the role assigned to him by his treacherous benefactor and his unfaithful beloved—the role of a child no longer deserving of his two parents' love, no doubt because he has desired them both too much—a child who has no right to anything anymore but to be beaten. And when he goes onstage the whole story gets dependably loud laughs from the public but also from him, the one who is beaten. For he is not a tragic Oedipus, Kofman writes, who tears out his eyes, but a clown who no longer takes anything or anyone seriously: not science, not the search for truth that he used to think sublime; not himself or the greats of this world, the grownups, the parents. They are all clowns; finally he has understood; nothing and no one can ever make him weep again.

He plays the role of a silly who tries to proclaim the truth—to no avail, because every time he tries to speak some other silly slaps him—and who tries proclaiming lies instead, with the same result: slaps. And the members of his audience—who are happily spared the trouble of ever believing in anything or recognizing the superiority of anyone—laugh. A clown cannot know the truth, there is no truth for a clown. So he has no right to speak, no right to anything but slaps until he is dead. Each evening the clown dies and is buried onstage for the greater enjoyment of the spectators who get to believe, at least as long as the show lasts, that they are superior to the clown whose very death is a joke; they get to believe that they will not be beaten or mocked, that they will not die. Their laughable laughter recalls the guffaws of the academicians, those so-called Immortals, actually an assembly of buffoons.

The clown's Oedipus is not tragic, then, Kofman says: rather it is a comedy that mocks mother and father and all humanity into the bargain. All humanity with its mysterious riddles and its pretensions. Its academies, its universities. For what does truth matter? Whether the earth is round or flat, it keeps on going round. And if you prefer not to despair, then you just help keep it going—round and round. And laugh at the folly involved in claiming to have any right to speak, any right to be a man.

If humor can imply such contempt for self and for all others, then it is easy to see why it is not for everyone. Still, those who have never felt the sting of their own scorn may well prove to be stuck in their self-satisfaction—as at an impasse or in a trap—barred from the daring lightheartedness of humor. It is not the happily sated Poros, after all, as Kofman points out, but the humiliated Penia who contrives her way out of a jam. Poros might never have had the clever thought of loving anything but himself, and thus remained sterile—which is to say, stymied. Anyway, the capacity to make oneself the object of one's own scorn and to laugh at one's own expense is said by Freud to be the precondition for making jokes. Kofman emphasizes this in *Pourquoi rit-on?* where she comments at length on *Jokes and Their Relation to the Unconscious*, citing Freud more than once to the effect that Jews, unparalleled in their flair as tellers of jokes, are predisposed to joke because of their double personality.[10] They not only think highly of themselves and ill of many others; they are also first among those others whom they judge harshly and scorn—and this doubleness is what makes them so well suited for joking. Indeed, this doubleness is among the features that Kofman stresses in her short book on Nietzsche and anti-Semitism, *Le mépris des Juifs*—a book that, I think, demonstrates her rather terrifying predilection for double-edged instruments: for stratagems, expedients dangerous to her to just the extent that they are salutary.[11]

In *Le mépris des Juifs*, she brings out in Nietzsche's writing a series of interrelated Jewish "inventions"—divine chosenness, an utterly transcendent law, and sin, ineradicable human sin—that form, as she puts it, a "system," and as such make "the Jew" an ambivalent, paradoxical figure: two-faced. On the one hand, he maintains a very elevated image of himself, as chosen by God and bearer of a sublime law. This enables him to greet scorn with scorn, scoffing at the contempt relentlessly shown him through the centuries with such robust persistence that Nietzsche exclaims the "heroism" of Jews "in the practice of *spernare se spernii* outshines the virtues of all the saints." On the other hand, as bearers of a law they can only ever fall short of, and which puts them forever at fault, they scorn themselves and hate themselves more than any other people has ever done. "This 'good' and this 'bad' self-image, Kofman writes, "give the Jew a double countenance" (Kofman 1994b, 40).

It is thanks to his two-facedness that he is so apt a teller of jokes—so apt, that is, at making himself and his entire people the target of his own witticisms—as in the following joke, the only one, actually, that I ever heard Sarah Kofman tell.

Jehovah, in search of a people to be the keeper of his law, approached one very strong and dignified people, and proposed that they be his elect and preserve his law, to which they responded by asking, what does it involve? Well, for example, thou shalt not kill, Jehovah said. Oh, that's not for us, the strong and dignified people said; so Jehovah approached another, almost as solid-and-respectable-looking people with the same proposition, that they be his chosen people and bearers of his law. Again they inquired what would be involved. And he answered, this time, thou shalt not, for example, commit adultery. Ah well, then, they replied, that would not be suitable for us. Finally, after several more tries, among less and less likely-looking candidates, Jehovah approached a very small and seedy people, the Hebrews, and proposed that they be his elect, and bear his law. How much is it? they asked. Well, it is free, Jehovah answered. Fine, they said. We'll take two.

In *Pourquoi rit-on?* Kofman wonders whether, by describing jokes as a Jewish specialty in *Jokes and Their Relation to the Unconscious*, and by mentioning as a specifically Jewish trait the doubleness that constitutes the precondition of jokes—and moreover by using Jewish jokes practically exclusively as examples—Freud may have been affirming a *Jewish* identity. Anti-Semites among his contemporaries were always denying that Jews had any identity at all. Instead Jews had, according to these bigots, a motley collection of character flaws. Freud's book on jokes, inasmuch as it counters this insult explicitly by suggesting that wit is specifically Jewish and that the Jewish people is a people of jokes, might, Kofman suggests, be considered profoundly militant and profoundly Jewish. But Freud did not by any means stress his own Jewishness in it. He said he was personally no good at telling jokes. He burned his collection of Jewish jokes after finishing *Jokes and Their Relation to the Unconscious*, and within that book, as Kofman stresses, he rather systematically de-emphasizes the specifically Jewish origin of the jokes he presents. He indicates that their Jewish character is really just part of their picturesque outer appearance—part of the charm whereby they capture the attention—and that their real point is simply human; it proceeds from a universal cynicism, and might be summed up by Horace's phrase, *carpe diem*: life is full of uncertainties, and there is nothing worth renouncing pleasure for when pleasure comes your way. Or, just underneath the civilized manners, the nice clothes, the noble values, there lies a far less edifying human nature, common to all and all too apt to show.

In fact, Freud's book on jokes might well, Kofman suggests, be the way he found to cease being a Jew altogether, while sparing himself the pain and guilt of converting and changing his name, like Heine. For if the Jew in *Jokes and Their Relation to the Unconscious* is described as a double personality, and featured as an exemplary maker of jokes, jokes—as though the better to forget about Jews—receive as their special emblem the two-faced Roman god Janus, the one always looking in two directions simultaneously, smiling in one, frowning in the other, who officiates at thresholds and portals, at passages and transitions of all kinds, laughing and scowling at the turn of the year, doing justice to the two moods of time, so to speak, the euphoric and the melancholic one.

In *Jokes and Their Relation to the Unconscious*, jokes are lodged under the sign of the two-faced god because jokes, Kofman writes, spare us misery by showing and mocking the two sides of everything, the yes and the no, the sense and the nonsense, without compromise and without ambiguity, but paradoxically, and playfully, with the *yes* and the irreconcilable *no* there both at once—the hilarity and the tears—as in a pun.

But so it is that the rascal *Witz* gets assimilated to a Roman deity. And Freud likewise, perhaps, pushed his own Jewish heritage into the background, the better to display his classical culture, his humanism, as a protection against misfortune, against anti-Semitism, against the dread of castration—not that he does not know that this protective Roman column, as Kofman puts it, is just the fetishist flip side of castration, apt at any moment to crumble, as if *it* had been the superficial outer appearance all along, and the Jewish origin behind it the actual point, just as many a joke teaches, in fact: the one Freud tells, for example, about the rich baroness in labor while her doctor and her husband play cards together outside her room. "*Ah mon Dieu que je souffre*," she cries, and her husband jumps to his feet, but the doctor does not even look up from the game. "There's no need to interrupt our evening yet," he says. An hour or so later: "*Mein Gott, mein Gott, was für Schmerzen*," the baroness moans. Again the husband leaps up, but the doctor remains unperturbed. Finally the doctor hears "*Oï Waïh, waïh*," at which point he rolls up his sleeves.

Maybe Freud covered up his Jewish face with his humanist one, his pagan one, but not without knowing all the same, Kofman says, that by so denying his debt to the Jewish tradition he acts just like the ne'er-do-well in the Jewish joke who blows the loan he has just extracted from a friend on a fancy lunch, explaining, "I certainly can't have salmon with mayonnaise when I'm poor, and if I can't have it when I'm flush, then when *am* I going to have it?" Freud is like this *Schnorrer* in that he does not seem to know the meaning of obligation, Kofman says (1986b, 47). Rather, he appears to think that between Jews there are no debts. In this belief he thinks like a pious Jew—and like the Pole in another joke who sits up when a stranger enters his train compartment, but sprawls out again when the stranger asks him how long it is till Yom Kippur. Perhaps Freud concealed his Jewish face behind a Roman one in his book on jokes; and yet thereby he refused the logic of Roman law according to which a debt must be remitted, and behaved, Kofman observes, like a faithful Jew who cannot possibly owe anything to other Jews or be owed anything by them. That is to say, Freud shows himself to be a skeptic *and* a religious man, both and irreducibly; he shows the double face of a pagan Jew, without apology, and it is in this way, Kofman suggests, that he does resemble double-visaged Janus. He does not fear contradiction. His double face does not have the neurotic structure of compromise; both visages are there at once, and even if one is valued more than the other, neither one's predominance enjoys stability; the hierarchy can always be reversed at a moment's notice, and reversed again (Kofman 1986b, 46–47).

It is interesting to notice, though, that Freud never does give the interpretation of the joke about the baroness in labor that I take for granted above. Kofman points out that Freud tells this joke twice, once at the beginning of *Jokes and Their Relation to the Unconscious* and once again at the end. The first time, he takes the joke to be on the baroness's pretensions, for she tries to appear more dignified and brave than she ultimately proves to be: when pain gets really bad, she reveals in spite of herself the primitive nature of humanity in general that civilization—expecting people to control themselves at all times—requires us to repress. When he proposes this interpretation, Freud takes the joke to be a genuine joke. At the end of his book, he proposes a different interpretation of it, and simultaneously demotes it from the status of a joke to that of a mere comic anecdote, the point of which would not have anything to do with mankind in general but would reveal, in all her earthiness, woman, and more precisely the mother, whom Freud enjoys degrading, Kofman observes, and laughing at and exposing to the laughter of his readers, presumed to be male. He never does make anything of the Jewish specificity of this joke, or anecdote—he never mentions that it is a humble Jewish origin that gets discovered underneath the baroness's layers of culture, and Kofman suggests that Freud must have preferred to gloss over this aspect of the story lest he reveal thereby his own laughable imposture, which consisted in concealing castration by means of a Roman costume—covering up his feminine or Jewish face with his double Janus visage (1986b, 196–97).

And yet, this is no doubt too simple an understanding, Kofman says. For the *Oï waïh* joke, or anecdote, also teaches that if the face of a man is never simple, it is not ever just double either. It is never just comprised of the dignified, civilized visage, plus the repressed, primitive one. Rather, it is triple: which is to say that if to be Jewish is first of all to be a man, to be a man is also, necessarily, at some level, the deepest, to be a Jew. Thus, Kofman writes, the impostors are not Jews who present themselves as men, but men who deny that in all men there is castration. If Freud burned his collection of Jewish jokes, and merged the substance of Jewish wit with that of a generalized human cynicism, it was the better to generalize this Jewish "identity" and to confer it upon the whole of humanity, and to relieve the entire species forever thereby of its secure, its certain, its one identity (1986b, 197).

Kofman's commentary on Freud's joke book, ending thus upon the thought of a Jewish "identity" putting identity itself into doubt, resonates with the hypotheses developed by her friends Philippe Lacoue-Labarthe and Jean-Luc Nancy in the essay they entitled "Le peuple juif ne rêve pas" (1981). They suggest that the question of Jewish identity may well have the capacity to shake something loose in the standard Freudian conceptions of identity and identification. Certainly it is true, they grant, that psychoanalysis places a huge, fundamental, determining emphasis on a massive identification with the father, and perhaps, they go on to surmise, it thereby only reconfirms and as it were compulsively reinforces the inevitability of totalitarianism as the fatal outcome of politics in the West. Yet it is conceivable that psychoanalysis also indicates a different problematic of identification and thus a different conception of politics. And if this is so, the deviation from the concepts and structures that take up the foreground in Freud's thought might lie in the general area of jokes and of the double personality of Jews—in the analysis of that "singular process which is the 'identification' of the Jewish people." The Jewish people does not dream, Nancy and Lacoue-Labarthe suggest. Its aptitude is not for the dream—that realm of simple, immediate identifications, of fusions and confusions in or with figures. The Jewish people does not identify, Lacoue-Labarthe and Nancy's theory goes, in dreams with the father—it does not adhere to the figure, the phantasm, or phantom of the father. If Judaism is indeed a religion of the father, it is so otherwise than via fusion with or in a paternal figure, for the special aptitude of the Jewish people is for jokes, not dreams. And jokes, quite unlike dreams that are strictly asocial, have a collective structure. The delight one derives from a joke involves telling it to someone else. Jokes are, as Freud emphasizes, the most social of any psychic activity aiming at pleasure. If the dream is the realm of simple, immediate identifications, jokes, on the other hand, by virtue of their sociality, engage us, Nancy and Lacoue-Labarthe argue, in more complex patterns, where identity becomes problematic. The Jewish people, a people more apt to joke than dream, furnishes a *social* paradigm of the process of identification.

The dream, however, is the royal road of psychoanalysis. So the analysis of the Jewish people might well require the pursuit of some other, not-so-royal road. It might require a path crossing into collective psychology. This detour—the way of *Moses and Monotheism*, for example—is liable, Nancy and Lacoue-Labarthe suggest, to bring psychoanalysis back to a Jewish heritage and identity, and in so doing to lead analysis out of itself and beyond any *identifiable* Jewishness. For this way—not the royal one—would necessarily head beyond the identity principle.

Kofman emphasizes the contrast between dreams and jokes, just as Nancy and Lacoue-Labarthe do. It is a contrast that Freud introduces belatedly in *Jokes and Their Relation to the Unconscious*, after a long analysis of the characteristics that dreams and jokes have in common, but it actually undermines, Kofman maintains, all the analogies initially elaborated. The contrast is between the profound narcissism of dreams and the collective dimension of jokes, which are social productions. If dreams and jokes both aim to outdo the censorship of the conscious mind the better to free unconscious thoughts, jokes, since they are told to another person—another watchful, conscious mind—cannot proceed in quite the same way that dreams do. Dreams benefit, as it were, from the suspended vigilance of the sleeping consciousness.

They can overcome inhibitions by means of compromise formations, wherein primary and secondary processes each concede something to the other. Jokes face a more alert and less permissive censor. Moreover, they must be intelligible to the very consciousness that they must also slip past, for the sake of the unconscious thoughts it ordinarily blocks. Whereas dreams cannot afford to be too easily understood (they would wake the dreamer if their meaning were too clear), the joke will fail if the person to whom it is told does not get it. So the joke must serve two masters at once, the conscious and the unconscious mind. This is the point that Kofman underscores. The joke must play on two different terrains at the same time. And it proceeds not through compromise formations of the type that characterize dreams, but like a "veritable Janus," by showing its two separate faces simultaneously, and blinding the censor with the dazzle of its double language.[12] Thus, in Kofman's thinking the paradoxical logic of jokes joins the more general essence of art and of laughter, which is that of the double—diabolically unidentifiable, wreaking havoc in the system that opposes appearance to reality, surface to depth, and so on. Painting, for example, introduces in between the real and the unreal an uncategorizable region, she says, inhabited by beings neither present nor absent, but whose absence is dense, intrusive, and whose presence is disquietingly remote. These ghost inhabitants of this unnamable region play, she writes, on two terrains at once, like all doubles. Like jokes. They show surface and depth at once, and belong to neither. They dis-figure every figure, causing everything that otherwise could have passed for an autonomous, self-sufficient presence to differ, to turn strange and unidentifiable. They are uncanny, petrifying. But they are *also* in league with laughter, which, Kofman writes, wrings meaning's neck and opens a space of indetermination.[13]

One might associate them with Baubô, lifting up her skirts, as Kofman recounts, showing what neither shows nor does not show, the better to get grieving Demeter to remember her fecundity and laugh.[14] Or with Eros, that demonic, intermediary being whom I evoked at the beginning of this chapter. Eros opens up the one way out for humans, Kofman writes—the one way out of the worst aporia, mortality. For the logic of love—the logic of the intermediary and not of identity—defeats all aporias. Humanity's one *poros* is neither Poros, then, nor Penia but Eros, whose ingenious expedient to get us past death is procreation, our *ersatz* immortality.[15] Sarah Kofman knew how to benefit from Eros' ingenuity. She was one of Nietzsche's children, who did not claim to have understood him but just to have lived with him and been continuously made fertile by him, all the while impregnating him, too, at least a little—displacing him somewhat, that is, from himself within himself, thanks to her Freudian ear.[16] For she always played Nietzsche and Freud together, the one against the other, as she said, lest either one lack for the traveling companion or guide—the friend, the rival double—for want of whom the tyrannical soul, the master, identical to himself, hits a snag despite all his resources, and becomes sterile. All he can do is frantically demand that everyone understand him.

Notes

The translations provided are the author's, except when indicated otherwise.

1. Similarly, in Kofman 1986b, 142 Kofman writes that the most acute pleasure in wordplay lies not so much, as is usually thought, in play itself, as in outplaying censorship.

2. Kofman's *Quatre romans analytiques* is translated as *Freud and Fiction* (1991).

3. Here I am thinking of Kofman's *Nietzsche et la scène philosophique*, especially the chapter entitled "Le masque de la sérénité" (Kofman 1979, 59–97), and in the chapter entitled "Baubô, perversion théologique et fétichisme" (293–97).

4. See "Le double e(s)t le diable," Kofman's study of Hoffmann's *Sandman* and of Freud's reading of that story, in Kofman 1974, 138–76; see Kofman 1991, 119–62 for the English translation.

5. Kofman quotes Freud's "Humor" in Kofman 1983b, 114 and in Kofman 1985a, 55, and Kofman 1980, 66. In Kofman 1974, 17; translation, 1991, 6 she quotes "Creative Writers and Daydreaming" to exactly the same effect.

6. See Kofman 1985a, 55–56.

7. See Kofman 1983b, 99–114.

8. See Kofman, 1987a.

9. See Kofman 1995a, 131–37.

10. Kofman 1986b. See, for example, p. 26.

11. See Kofman 1994b.

12. See Kofman 1986b, 131–33.

13. See "La mélancolie de l'art," in Kofman 1985b, 11–33, esp. 17–18.

14. Kofman discusses Baubô in Kofman 1979, 263–304. An English translation of this essay, by Tracy B. Strong—"Baubô: Theological Perversion and Fetishism"—appeared in *Nietzsche's New Seas: Explorations in Philosophy, Aesthetics and Politics*, ed. Michael Allen Gillespie and Tracy B. Strong (Chicago: University of Chicago Press, 1988), 175–202.

15. See Kofman 1986a, 64–69.

16. Kofman includes herself among Nietzsche's children, and evokes her life with him, in the last pages—the "Supplément rhapsodique"—of *Explosions II* (1993).

PART II

Philosophical Fires: Autobiography, Femininity, and Jewishness

CHAPTER 4

Fire Walls: Sarah Kofman's Pyrotechnics

MICHAEL NAAS

Prometheus

She was in her own way Promethean. Though it may seem a rather odd epithet to pin on this somewhat diminutive, fragile, and in many ways vulnerable woman, who, in going up against the gods did so in a bold and courageous but always nonflamboyant manner, Sarah Kofman was nonetheless, though always in her own way, Promethean. She was Promethean, as I will try to show, in her ruses and in her strategies, in her wit and in her craft, and, as the name "Pro-metheus" suggests, in her foresight and her forethought, knowing from the very beginning, I think, just how to become what she already was. She was Promethean in her suffering, shackled to a traumatic childhood in wartime Paris, where, at the age of seven, she would see her father, Rabbi Berek Kofman, taken from their apartment on the rue Ordener and sent off, as she would later learn, to die at Auschwitz. Like Prometheus, then, whose liver was eaten away by a bird of misfortune by day and made to grow back by night, Sarah Kofman had to endure the eternal return of this traumatic past, a nightly and often nightmarish visitation that would reopen the wounds that had been partially healed during the day by the practices of writing and philosophy, her way, as we will see, of trying to make the intolerable tolerable. Like Prometheus, Sarah Kofman was haunted in her dreams by just such a bird of misfortune, whether eagle or vulture, and just as with Prometheus it was on the liver that this recurring trauma was played out, the liver being the mirror, as Sarah Kofman well knew from her reading of Plato's *Timaeus*, where our pains and desires come to be reflected in dreams (see Kofman 1999). She was Promethean, therefore, in her suffering and in the strategies she deployed to alleviate that suffering, knowing full well that the only way to make the intolerable tolerable, to get the intolerable past Zeus or the censor of dreams, was to dress it up, and, as Hesiod tells the story in the *Theogony*, pass one sacrifice off for another, a ruse that would ultimately lead Zeus to take back from man the power of fire, so necessary for the arts and human culture.

And so Sarah Kofman was eminently Promethean in this too, in her theft of fire out of love for humankind, Prometheus being called in Aeschylus's *Prometheus Bound* a most philanthropic god (l.11.122), just as Socrates, the figure to whom Kofman would devote one of her last books, is said at *Euthyphro* 3d to be the most philanthropic of men. She stole fire from Zeus just like Prometheus, not outright, in the open, since this would have been doomed to failure, but cunningly, concealing it in her flight from Olympus in "a hollow fennel stalk" that, we might speculate, looked at bit like her father's fountain pen—the only thing she possessed in her later years of her father, the fountain pen that provides the opening image of her extraordinary autobiography, *Rue Ordener, rue Labat*.

Yes, Sarah Kofman was, however odd the sobriquet, Promethean, though always in her own way, in *her* own way, which means that in her case we cannot exclude from the Promethean legend either Prometheus's forgetful brother, Epimetheus, or the fateful Pandora whom Epimetheus brought to mankind. We cannot forget that it was because of this theft of fire that Zeus sent as punishment to mankind the poisoned gift of Pandora, from whom was born "the race of women and female kind" (Hesiod 1943, 590), a work of pure guile that was accepted by the forgetful, backward-looking Epimetheus, much to the dismay of the forward-looking, all too forward-looking Prometheus. Though the moral of these tales of Prometheus in Hesiod's *Theogony* and *Works and Days* is that "it is not possible to deceive or go beyond the will of Zeus," Kofman would devote her life to showing that there are ways to escape the constraints of the gods or the bonds of Necessity without necessarily escaping them, ways that teach us how to use our intelligence not to avoid but to track, multiply, and embrace these aporia as the only way of twisting free from them, the best way of making the intolerable tolerable.[1] The Promethean Kofman would teach us how to use our gifts, all our gifts, including the gifts of guile that go by the name of Pan-dora, to escape an intolerable situation, and, perhaps for a moment, get "beyond aporia."

In the work of Sarah Kofman, the guile used by Father Zeus to punish humankind is turned against the father and his authority, fire being used to fight fire. Fire flares up from the ashes throughout her life and her corpus, and perhaps especially from her two great books on Nietzsche's quasi-autobiography, *Ecce Homo*, where a brilliant reading of the conflagration that was Nietzsche's thought is combined with an occasional, always strategic reference to that intolerable conflagration that was the Holocaust, or, as she would prefer to call it, "Auschwitz." Entitled *Explosion I* (1992) and *Explosion II* (1993) these two books, written near the end of her life, this single book divided into two volumes, these two explosions, these two great bodies of smoldering words, begin by recalling that, for Nietzsche, thinking could be a kind of fire, a conflagration that can be turned against the worst, against the all-consuming flame, to make—at least for a time—the intolerable tolerable.[2] Though always discreet, a master of pyrotechnics, of the controlled burn, a thinker and writer who never gave in, at least not in her writing, to flamboyance or bombast, Sarah Kofman was such a force and such a conflagration. Like Prometheus, she used this force and this fire to contest the authority of all authorities, and, like Freud, to diagnose in us not only the fires of our passion and creativity but our most destructive impulses.

And so in all these ways—in her cunning and intelligence, her suffering and her love, her theft of fire and her commitment to use the gifts of the paternal gods against the gods themselves, against our gods and against the gods in us, in order to help us too to see that there is a Necessity to which not only we but also those gods must submit—Sarah Kofman was in her own way Promethean. And she was Promethean, finally, because she was a philosopher, Prometheus being called in *Comment s'en sortir?* the "first philosopher." Though Gaston Bachelard claimed in the *Psychoanalysis of Fire* (1968, 24) that Prometheus, identified with the erotic imagery of fire, was a "vigorous lover rather than an intelligent philosopher," Kofman, as a student of Plato, knew that these two traits can coincide in the philosopher, and Sarah Kofman was, perhaps before all else, a philosopher, one whose extraordinary passion and erudition allowed her to write with authority on figures ranging from the pre-Socratics (particularly Empedocles and Heraclitus), to Plato and Aristotle, to Enlightenment figures like Kant, Rousseau, and Diderot, to twentieth-century thinkers such as Sartre, Blanchot, and Derrida.

In what follows, I will restrict myself for the most part to Kofman's reading of Plato, for Sarah Kofman was, as we know, a great and innovative teacher of Plato and, in a couple of works, a dynamite reader of him. Speaking of the conversion by which Kofman throughout her life turned life against death, Françoise Proust once wrote that "in order to operate this conversion, Sarah Kofman turned three levers: Nietzsche, Freud, and, paradoxically, Plato" (1997, 57).[3] "Paradoxically," writes Proust, because Nietzsche's archenemy was, in so many ways, Plato, and sometimes even Socrates, the life-denying, talkative Socrates who reveals his contempt for life in his dying words to Crito, "We owe a cock to Asclepias." Plato and Socrates, then, Plato as the disciple of Socrates, the disciple who perhaps had to turn against the father as the best way of being faithful to him—an interpretation Kofman herself offers in the first chapter of her *Socrates: Fictions of a Philosopher* (1998). For Kofman, so much will have begun with Socrates and Plato. In a text written after Kofman's death, Jacques Derrida recalls the day he first met Sarah Kofman as she came to his office at the Ecole normale supérieure "to tell [him], among other things, that she protested or objected to something [he] had ventured in

Plato's Pharmacy" (Derrida 2001, 183). Kofman surely knew that in protesting in this way she was affirming everything Derrida said in that work about philosophy and parricide. She surely knew all that but also knew, in some sense, that her life would be inseparable from her philosophy, the most abstract philosophy never being completely distinguishable from the family scene, complete with its own parricides. Whether she was reading Plato's *Symposium*, Diderot's *The Nun*, or Nietzsche's *Ecce Homo*, Sarah Kofman could not help but catch a glimpse of herself—or, perhaps, of a double she could never completely know. Indeed, that is how I will propose reading the opening and closing pages of Kofman's only book devoted entirely to Plato, so as to give some small indication of how this book, like all those Kofman wrote, is less a thesis or a reading than a tightly woven stratagem, a dense tissue of citation and ruse, containing an ineluctable autobiographical element, one that begins by looking like a psychoanalytic interpretation of individual desire but ends up affirming the whole of what is through the *amor fati*. By means of this brief tour through the opening and closing pages of *Comment s'en sortir?* (1983a), translated into English as "Beyond Aporia?" (1988a), I hope to show how Kofman reads not just Plato but any thinker, and to give some indication of how I think we should read Kofman—namely, with care, strategy, love, and foresight (like a good Promethean), knowing all along that we may be overlooking what is truly essential, right before our eyes, since the very condition of our Promethean sight is our Epimethean blindness, the price of our theft of fire the ashes in our eyes.[4]

Aporia

If all Kofman's books are strategies, intricate ruses, *Comment s'en sortir?* is strategic and full of ruses in an exemplary way. Like Pandora's box, it has to be opened with caution, without forgetting to read the label, since the wrapping is, as always, part of the gift: *Comment s'en sortir?* How to get out of this? The phrase in French asks not simply how to get out of something we know already has an exit, even if we do not yet know where that exit is; it asks not *comment sortir?* but how to get out of what we already know is a difficult situation, a jam, an aporia—*Comment s'en sortir?* Yet because, as we will see, the way out is precisely through the right kind of aporia, the way out being inseparable from the way in which we are riveted, immobilized, bound like Prometheus, we are invited to hear *Comment s'en sortir?* as *Comment sans sortir? Comment s'en sortir sans sortir?* How, in not getting out, are we to get out? And if this homonymic play seems fanciful, let me recall that already back in 1929 Max Ernst—a surrealist artist whose work I have reason to believe Kofman knew quite well—used it in his collection *La femme 100 têtes*, that is, "the woman with a hundred heads [cent têtes]," "the woman with bloodied heads [sang têtes]," "the woman without a head [sans têtes]," "the headstrong woman [s'entête]."[5] The title is thus already a trap, already an aporia for any translator tempted to choose one meaning over another; like the word "aporia" itself, as Kofman will go on to demonstrate, the title is untranslatable: ruse number one.

Now, if the question of the title is "how to get out of this fix, this jam," the epigraph from Blanchot's *Madness of the Day* begins to answer the question of what it is we, or humankind, want to get out of. A line from this quasi-autobiographical text of Blanchot reads, "Men would like to escape death, strange species." In the reading of Plato, and particularly the *Symposium*, that follows, Kofman will analyze Plato's answer to the question of how our strange species tries to escape from death, how it attempts to gain a measure of immortality usually reserved only for the gods. The answer, of course, turns out to be Love, Eros, procreation in either body or soul, though preferably in soul, preferably in philosophy—an answer that Kofman will not, on my reading, outright reject but will inflect in her own Promethean way from the very first page on.

Kofman thus begins the first chapter, entitled "Poros, son of Metis," with what initially appears to be a traditionally scholastic gesture, that is, with a reference to a master text in Greek studies in France, Marcel Detienne and Jean-Pierre Vernant's classic work *Cunning Intelligence in Greek Culture and Society* (1978). She begins, "Marcel Detienne and Jean-Pierre Vernant conclude their remarkable study of the *metis* of the Greeks . . ." (1988a, 8). Kofman begins, therefore, with seeming deference to two masters, acknowledging her enormous debt to them and their work. But it does not take long for the Promethean Kofman to begin, discreetly though unmistakably, to distance herself from the essential thesis of this book by supplementing it with another concerning the aporia in Plato's work. If the thesis of Detienne and Vernant's classic book is that philosophy, in the name of "Truth," excluded the kind of cunning intelligence that works by means of stratagems and detours, Kofman will add that philosophy did so only at the price of using and then forgetting those very stratagems and detours so as to bring about that exclusion. That is, if philosophy condemned all kinds of uncertain, oblique, or obscure procedures by opposing them to the exact, rigorous, philosophical *epistēmē*, it did so only by using the techniques it condemned.

Kofman can thus begin by saying that Detienne and Vernant's thesis is, as far as it goes, "irrefutable and classical" (1983a, 8). Philosophy would indeed be that form of knowledge that decides what is true or legitimate and what is not. Everything associated with *metis*, such as sophistry and rhetoric, would thus appear to be excluded and condemned by Plato in no uncertain terms, or rather, to use the words of Detienne and Vernant, "without any equivocation [sans aucune ambiguité]." But with this first quote from *Cunning Intelligence* Kofman begins to take her distance from it. After saying that "this conclusion seems irrefutable and classical," Kofman begins the very next paragraph with an "and yet [*et pourtant*]"—reminiscent of, or actually, I think, a cunning echo of, one of those "and yets" commented upon and used by Derrida in a text Kofman knew so well, *The Truth in Painting*, "and yets" that themselves echoed Heidegger's "*und dennoch*"s in "The Origin of the Work of Art" and that, curiously, anticipate Derrida's not yet published text entitled "Khôra," a work on Plato that itself begins with a quote from none other than Detienne and Vernant.[6]

> And yet if philosophy could not do without *metis*, if its "contemplative" understanding did not make a radical break with "technical" understanding, perhaps Plato's gesture would not be so simple or so unequivocal—even if (and here she affirms the essential thesis of Vernant and Detienne once again) it cannot be denied that he does make a hierarchical distinction between philosophy and other sciences, between philosophy and *technē*, between philosophy and sophistry (Kofman 1988a, 8).

Notice, Kofman is not claiming, as some might too quickly conclude, that the dramatic form of Plato's dialogues, along with Plato's use of irony, rhetoric, and myth, serve strategically to overturn the hierarchies that are seemingly established in the dialogues between philosophy and its others. Hierarchies *are* indeed claimed in Plato; philosophy *is* set over sophistry and rhetoric; science *is* seen as superior to *metis*. And yet, in excluding the latter in favor of the former, Plato's gesture is not without equivocation or ambiguity—either because he himself saw the necessity of ruse and cunning as the very means to setting up the sovereignty of philosophy or because his dialogues reveal that in any attempt to exclude ruse and cunning the excluded or repressed always returns and remains recoverable by a deconstructive reading.

This is how Kofman treats philosophers and philosophy, how she deals here with the philosopher Plato and with Vernant and Detienne's treatment of him. Kofman's rereading of Plato on the authority of philosophy is thus closely bound up with her contestation of two authorities on the role of philosophy in ancient Greece. In neither case does Kofman deny anything; indeed, she affirms the explicit theses of both Plato and Detienne and Vernant, but she then goes on to show that in Plato's hierarchies and Detienne and Vernant's analyses of them a fundamental ambiguity has been forgotten, repressed, and marginalized, and so needs to be recovered. In her implicit reading of Vernant and Detienne, it is the "equivocation" or "ambiguity" of what seemed to be Plato's simple, straightforward gesture of exclusion that needs to be recovered. In Plato, this will be the ambiguity—the double aporia, in fact—hidden in the myth of Eros as Plato gives it to us in the *Symposium*. Kofman thus makes way for a recovery of the essential, structural ambiguity of the figure of Penia, the mother of Eros, a figure of the philosopher, by recovering the ambiguity neglected by Detienne and Vernant's masterful but still forgetful, Epimethean reading of Plato. So much for Kofman's uncritical reverence for father figures. Kofman thus thanks Detienne and Vernant, acknowledges her debt to them, and cites them, but then, on the basis of that citation, begins to show how they, in their focus on the exclusion of *metis* in Plato, uncritically repeated a Platonic exclusion of ambiguity, an exclusion that, already in Plato, was not without ambiguity.

Penia-Aporia

Kofman then announces her own point of departure: "I will begin with the celebrated myth of the birth of Love in *The Symposium*."[7] In her only book devoted solely to Plato, Kofman begins not with the theory of Forms, not with a discussion of anamnesis or imitation or participation, not with the distinction between mythos and logos, but with a myth and, more particularly, a myth about origins. She begins with what she calls Socrates or Diotima's "genealogical fantasy [généalogie fantastique]" (1988a, 8), with the myth of Eros born to a father named Poros (Resource), the son of Metis, and a mother named Penia (Poverty), in order to question the family origins of philosophy.[8]

Kofman thus attempts in her reading of the Socrates-Diotima myth to show how philosophy, through the figure of Eros, has an ancestry both in Poros, in resourcefulness—and so in Metis, the mother of Poros—as well as in Penia, in poverty, a poverty or resourcelessness that will ultimately prove to be fundamentally ambivalent, being both poverty and resourcefulness, barrenness and fecundity. Kofman's emphasis on the ancestry of Eros supports in a dramatic and succinct way her thesis that philosophy can never completely condemn or banish *metis*, or ruse, without ambiguity. By giving philosophy an ancestry in Metis, Plato is actually associating philosophy with all the arts or *technai* that, on Detienne and Vernant's account, were condemned by philosophy in the name of knowledge or *epistēmē*. In other words, philosophy is now related—literally related—to those forms of thought that allow us "to discover *poroi* that can free man from aporia, from all sorts of difficult situations from which there is no way out" (1988a, 9). Though Plato condemns the techniques of the sophist or rhetorician, these techniques are nonetheless "*incorporated* by the philosopher," swallowed whole by him, just as Zeus was forced to swallow Metis in order to maintain his mastery over her and her progeny.[9]

Yet Kofman's reading of the Socrates-Diotima myth in the *Symposium* is even more intent on pointing out and clarifying the fundamental ambivalence of philosophy's maternal side. Through a careful reading of the myth, Kofman shows how Penia, the mother of Eros, and thus of the philosopher, is so impoverished that she does not even have an ancestry in the myth, though she turns out to be just as resourceful, if not more so, than Poros, the resourceful son of Metis. For we will recall that in this myth, as told by Socrates, Penia, or poverty, was not invited to the banquet of the gods honoring the birth of Aphrodite. Poros, or Resource, was invited, but ended up imbibing so much nectar that he wandered off from the banquet into a garden and fell into a stupor. Seeing his vulnerability, Penia hatched the plot to have a child by the sleeping Poros, Penia here showing the ruse and resourcefulness of Poros, and Poros being reduced through sleep to Penia. From the union of Poros and Penia was thus born Eros, a figure compared throughout the *Symposium* to Socrates, who is seen as being himself in aporia, himself a walking aporia, a demonic figure who throws others into aporia while, in the end, offering them a way out—a little bit of immortality through love or desire for beautiful objects, whether of body or of soul.

Like Eros, then, Socrates would be not a god but a sort of daimon, an intermediary between the human and the divine, between divine knowledge and human ignorance. Like his mother, he would be lacking in knowledge, and yet, as the word "philosophy" implies, desirous of it, aware of what he lacks and so not completely ignorant. "Neither ignorant nor knowing" (Kofman 1988a, 26)—or, as Kofman translates the Greek into French, "ni ignorant ni savant," this translation being a word-for-word citation of the opening line of *The Madness of the Day*, the quasi-autobiographical text by Blanchot used in the epigraph, a text whose narrator resembles, according to Kofman, not only Socrates but Oedipus.[10] Knowing that he does not know, desirous therefore to know, Socrates, like Eros, excites in others a desire to procreate, to touch immortal things and have a share in them.

Indeed, as Plato presents it, that is the work of philosophy, a work that makes our intolerable mortality tolerable; by procreating, or by creating works of art, laws, and cities, we are given a share of immortality reserved only for the gods. It is precisely here that Kofman will, all the while affirming this work of philosophy, just as she affirmed the work of Detienne and Vernant, uncover or recover an ambivalence lodged at the heart of the philosophical project, an ambivalence to be found more in its matrilineal than in its patrilineal heritage. For *that*, in the end, was the "true" work of the philosopher named Sarah Kofman: to expose the aporias—I would be tempted to call them the eternal, immortal aporias—upon which all philosophical edifices are founded, not, as one might think, to bring an end to philosophy but precisely to renew it, to rekindle it from its ashes, to give it new life in order to overcome, or make tolerable, the aporias of madness and death.

In Penia, we have a sort of condensation of poverty, resourcefulness, and aporia, a confusion of the male and female lines. Which means that we do an injustice to terms like *poros* and *aporia* each time we translate them in a way that completely excludes, without any ambiguity, their contraries. In a devilish little parenthetical aside, Kofman speaks of the genuine aporia translators find themselves in when having to translate these words in a way that does justice to their rich semantic field and that makes the relationship between, say, *poros* (usually translated as resource, means, or expedient) and *aporia* (often translated as resourcelessness) as audible in French or English as it is in Greek. To translate these words of ruse and expedience, one needs more than just a bit of cunning oneself, along with an awareness that any solution, any invention, will involve some form of betrayal. Kofman writes: "To translate, to open up a path through a language by using its resources, to decide upon *one* meaning, is to escape the agonizing, aporetic impasses of any translation, to make the philosophical gesture *par excellence*: the gesture of betrayal" (1988a, 9; italics in the original). The gesture is always one of betrayal, because what is betrayed in translation, in the translation of a word like *aporia*, is the aporia, the ambivalence—indeed, the "structural ambivalence"—of such a word in favor of a logic of the either/or, either this meaning or that one. When we recognize this about translation, when we recognize that our language has resources that cannot be so easily reduced to one meaning or another, we begin to disrupt or—since Kofman often used the word—"deconstruct" at once an ontology or epistemology that relied upon the reduction of ambivalence and a philosophy of translation that went hand in hand with it. Kofman continues: "To recognize the untranslatability of *poros* and *aporia* is to indicate that there is something about the terms, which Plato borrows from a whole tradition, that breaks with a philosophical conception of translation, and with the logic of identity that it implies" (9–10).

Such is the parenthetical expedience Kofman resorts to in order to explain aporia, recovering at once the aporias of Plato's philosophy and the aporetic nature of many of its terms, beginning with *aporia*. This is a pretty good stratagem; Kofman has, without finding the perfect translation for *aporia*, escaped for a time the dilemma by explaining the nature of that dilemma and, implicitly, criticizing the naïveté involved in not recognizing it. Like Socrates, she is neither knowing nor ignorant; she does not know how to translate *aporia*, or, for that matter, *poros*, but she knows that she does not know. She has exposed the aporia of *aporia*, and she has shown us one way out, one way among others, one path, even if it remains provisional, a *poros* rather than a *hodos*, a strategy rather than a method, an expedient that will have to be reinvented the next time rather than a formula to be repeated.

And so, in the course of her analysis of the *Symposium* in *Comment s'en sortir?* Kofman recovers from Plato's text the fundamental ambivalence of this female figure Penia, which she sees as being so aporetic that she writes her name at one point Penia-Aporia, Penia-Aporia as the mother of Eros, and thus the mother of philosophy, Penia-Aporia as the one who, in devising a plan to have a child, the child who will make it possible for humankind to participate in immortality, shows herself to be resourceful in and through her poverty. Though Eros will ultimately be the fruit of Penia-Aporia, Eros who will motivate the climb up the ladder of love, who will animate the drive to reduce all ambivalence or equivocation through intelligibility and philosophy, he will be forever marked by Penia-Aporia, by his untranslatable, ungraspable, ambivalent, intermediary mother. Even though Penia-Aporia might appear from the very beginning to be big with Eros, with a philosophical (rather than a sophistical) aporia that will lead mankind out of ambivalence and into a realm of univocal meaning, she will forever threaten the meanings she makes possible. "That is why," Kofman writes, "Aporia, which breaks with the logic of identity, and which pertains to the logic of the intermediary, is an untranslatable term" (1988a, 27).

As the mother of Eros, himself an intermediary, Penia-Aporia breaks with the logic of identity, which is also the logic of reason and of immortality. Penia-Aporia, mother of Eros, can thus never be dissociated from madness or from death, that is, from *thanatos*. In a little text entitled *Conversions*, Kofman returns again to the *Symposium* in order to uncover from within it yet another repressed aporetic figure, not quite Penia-Aporia but a related figure, a third Aphrodite, neither Aphrodite Ouranos nor Aphrodite Pandemos but a Chthonic Aphrodite, identical, as she says, to death, repressed by Pausanias, who divides this ambivalent figure into two opposed figures (see Kofman 1987a, 27, 46–47). By making such a division, by repressing the ambivalence of death and of meaning, philosophy makes the intolerable tolerable. It brings the intolerable into myth or into narrative and so transforms it into something now simply opposed to the tolerable.[11] Penia-Aporia is thus an intermediary figure between the mother who is already full with philosophical Eros, already on her way to being forgotten or repressed by philosophy as we move up the ladder of love from beautiful bodies to beautiful souls to the Beautiful itself, and the ambivalent mother who at once nurtures and devours. Penia-Aporia is thus doubly impoverished and doubly resourceful, neither nurturing mother nor devouring mother but both at once.

Maman-Mémé: The Family Scene

Penia-Aporia: one mother with two names, unless these two names, so closely related, suggest two mothers—like Maman and Mémé—the emphasis being put here on the ambivalence of the mother and the relative absence of the father, as if Kofman could not help but read her own family scene into that of the *Symposium*. Indeed, we all know the emphasis Kofman placed on the family scene, not only in her readings of Freud and Nietzsche, but in her own autobiographical works, such as *Rue Ordener, rue Labat*, where the appearance and disappearance of not just one but two mothers scans the very narrative and seems to be the measure of time itself. Penia (poverty) is always already an orphan, just as she, Sarah, would in effect become an orphan with the arrest of her father in 1942 and her stay with an adopted mother on the rue Labat. And if, to forestall any objections here, these autobiographical elements seem inappropriate for a reading of Kofman's interpretation of the *Symposium*, let me point out that it was Kofman herself who chose to append to this interpretation of Plato a short autobiographical text entitled simply "Nightmare," the presence of which has to be explained by any reading that wants to understand the overall strategy of this properly fascinating little text. And let me also recall Kofman's claim in *Socrates: Fictions of a Philosopher* that the various speeches in praise of Eros in the *Symposium*, just like the various readings of Socrates throughout the tradition, from Plato and Xenophon to Hegel, Kierkegaard, and Nietzsche, all entail—indeed, cannot but entail—a kind of narcissistic self-reflection or "fiction," as Kofman would call it, making every reading of the myth of Eros as much about the reader as about Eros.

It is thus not surprising that in following Kofman through the labyrinth of *Comment s'en sortir?* I am led to follow the figures of the family scene: as Deleuze would say in derision of the oedipal triangle, the figures of Mommy, Daddy, and Me. Had I the time, I would wish to show how Kofman treats each of these figures in her other texts: the theological figure of the father as artist and creator, the figure of the mother as the place of a fundamental ambivalence, and, finally, the figure of the self as a kind of narcissistic projection onto the screen of narrative. Already in her reading of the *Symposium*, Kofman calls the myth of Eros a "genealogical fantasy" on the part of Diotima and/or Socrates—"genealogical fantasy" being the very phrase used by Kofman to describe Nietzsche's attempts to rewrite his own past in *Ecce Homo* and elsewhere, his attempts to retrieve elements from the past so as to construct a fiction about that past.

But before showing how these figures crop up in several other Kofman texts, let me fill out the family scene of the *Symposium* and of Plato, as Kofman reads it, by adding to the oedipal triangle the figure of the sibling—the twin or rival brother. Because the philosopher, the figure of Eros or of Socrates, inherits not only poverty but resource from his parents, resource, paradoxically, from the cunning Penia-Aporia, he resembles to an almost maddening degree someone else who uses ruse and aporia for ends other than those of knowledge and truth. That other, that evil twin, is, of course, the sophist. Because the philosopher needs sophistry in order to exclude the sophist—after all, if the sophist were to listen to reason he would be a philosopher—the philosopher and the sophist turn out to be doubles, inextricably attached, a bit like Prometheus and Epimetheus, so much so, writes Kofman, that "the death of one signs the death warrant of the other." "No one," as she says, "resembles the sophist more closely than the philosopher" (1998a, 17), and so the following chapter of *Comment s'en sortir?* is devoted to showing how Plato tries to distinguish these two figures of aporia, the good and the bad, the one that can orient us toward a way out and the one that hurls us into the limitless and aporetic space that Plato likens to Tartarus—a chaos without bounds, the intolerable itself. Though it is not easy to tell the good aporia from the bad, the philosopher from the sophist, Socrates himself often being taken as a sophist by those who have not been stung by him, those who have not yet begun to feel their ignorance, to see their aporetic situation, the difference is essential. The operation proper to philosophical speculation is, for Plato, to separate the good aporia from the bad by opposing the upward path toward intelligibility and light to the downward path toward sensibility and obscurity.[12] Translated into the family scene, the work of philosophy is to distinguish the good brother from the bad. Kofman writes: "This is why, in order to safeguard reason from madness, and in order to master a mimesis that cannot, ultimately, be mastered, Plato makes a salutary distinction between good and bad mimesis, between noble and base sophistry, between dog and wolf; and this is why he attempts to distinguish between philosophical aporia and sophistical aporia, which are as alike as rival brothers" (1988a, 17). Philosophy not only tolerates but lives off this fraternal struggle; for what the bad brother makes the good one forget is the ambivalent mother that would petrify both. What is properly speaking intolerable for Plato is thus not the downward way, the bad aporia or the bad brother, but the place where good and bad cannot be distinguished, where each can be converted into the other, the place that disrupts the logic of identity—the place of Penia-Aporia, a place of madness and of death. Sibling rivalry, however fierce, keeps us from madness.

It would be possible, I believe, to follow this family scene through all of Kofman's works—for example, in her critique of the theological notion of the artist as genius or as creator in works such as *The Childhood of Art* (1988).[13] We would see there that Kofman, like Freud, refuses simply to reject all father figures as errors but wishes instead to diagnose them as illusions, illusions that offer us the only real means to their overcoming. Following both Freud and Nietzsche, Kofman attempts to unmask a conception of paternity and of artistic creation—a conception that is tainted by the theological model—so as to have a good laugh at all the emperors with no clothes. She writes, for example: "If life is the product of chance, the artist can no more be the father of his works than the father can be a God, or God be a father. For chance is one with necessity (*Ananke*) and stands opposed to finality, choice, the election of one being over another, endowed with exclusive and special gifts."[14] That we are not fundamentally the products of our parents, that we are not their chosen ones, that artists are essentially not the creators of their work, that all life and all creation are given over to chance, to an inscrutable Necessity, to the play of biological, psychical, and external forces, conflicting forces—that would be, in Kofman's eyes, precisely what an entire theological conception of paternity and artistic creativity has tried to repress. Art, like religion, consists of illusions, narcissistic projects designed to help us think that we are the masters of our fate, of our lives and of our deaths, masters over creation and procreation; it is designed to let us think we can assign and know origins (parents, the artist, God) when it is, in the end, life itself, this inscrutable—intolerable—play of forces that is the only origin, an intolerable origin that all our idolatry aims to overcome and render tolerable.

In *The Melancholy of Art* we learn that philosophy, the fascination of philosophical speculation, is yet another way, even more cunning perhaps than art or religion, of making the intolerable tolerable. For philosophy works not by denying the deadly fascination of the intolerable but by turning another form of fascination against it. In order to counter or escape the frightening fascination of the simulacrum, of images that come to compromise all identity, Plato in the *Republic*, *Sophist*, and elsewhere proposes the remedy of philosophy and its speculation. He does so not by abandoning simulacra but by reforming them, putting them into the service of philosophy and truth in order to turn them against their creators, like a Perseus who slays the Medusa by fascinating and petrifying her through her own reflection. Kofman writes: "Perseus was able to be victorious over the Medusa only by making her contemplate her own fascinating image in a mirror; philosophical speculation is such a mirror, receiving images much too powerful, much too intolerable. Without this speculation, philosophy and the philosopher would risk death or madness" (1985b, 20).

This is the pharmaceutical function of philosophy and of art, of theory and of theater. By turning a good form of mimesis against a bad, philosophy and art are able to transform into speculation and spectacle, into something bearable if not pleasurable, what is without them intolerable. For Plato, both philosophy and art must attempt to master the simulacrum and lead it to reasonable and productive ends (see Kofman 1985b, 27). Both must attempt to purify us of the intolerable threat of death or of madness.[15] Philosophy is just such a *garde-feu* or *garde-fou*, or, as my title indicated, just such a fire wall, and the only means it has or ever will have of fighting the conflagrations of madness or death is cunning, ruses that can turn the unmasterable forces of madness and death against themselves for a time—and to do so, for Kofman, in the name of life. Thus, while Plato might have tried to protect philosophy from, say, the fires of sophistry or the great conflagrations of Heraclitus by building a fire wall between philosophy and its others, a big fire-resistant wall designed to protect philosophy from the flames, ruse was needed in order to distract and co-opt these destructive forces, fire being needed to fight fire. And so, despite Plato's desire to protect philosophy, despite Vernant and Detienne's claim that philosophy could exclude ruse without ambiguity or equivocation, and so keep the forces of madness and death outside the citadel of truth, other kinds of fire walls were needed: not those made out of some repellent, fire-retardant material, something antithetical to fire itself, but, like those put into our software, fire walls made of the same materials as the viruses and Trojan horses they would protect us from, fire walls that simply try to outmaneuver and outtrick the viruses that try to trick them, in order to sneak in past the censor. Like Perseus's reflecting shield, these fire walls incorporate or build into the citadel of philosophy the very techniques and arts they would have liked to exclude without any ambiguity. Which is why the expert hacker is always the best builder of fire walls, the best philosopher the one able to construct the most cunning texts.

In each of her texts, Kofman tries to show the ways in which the forces of life—be they in art, religion, philosophy, or science—try to make the intolerable tolerable by reducing the intolerable both/and, the condition of all convertibility, to a tolerable either/or.[16] As a philosopher, as a Promethean, Sarah Kofman threw her lot in with these forces of life. Yet Kofman's ruse is to make the intolerable tolerable precisely by showing how others have effaced, forgotten, or sublated the intolerable. Her Promethean task was always to shine a light precisely on this conversion of the intolerable into the tolerable, never forgetting that she herself, in the name of philosophy, was doing something at once very similar and very different: using the light or fire of philosophy to turn it against itself, so as to show the aporia or conflagration upon which all philosophy rests, so as to uncover a repressed maternal line—philosophy's ancestry in Dionysus or in Penia-Aporia, in a mother who is double or duplicitous, not one thing at one moment and another at another but both at once.[17]

Mommy, Daddy, and Me—the oedipal triangle is certainly strained when the father is gone and the mother is unbearable: but what happens when Mommy is not only Maman but also Mémé? I recall that these two mothers—Sarah's biological mother, her Jewish mother, who lived on the rue Ordener, and her adopted mother, the Christian woman named Mémé who took her and her mother in at the rue Labat—would, in the years following the father's arrest, fight over Sarah, whose early life is literally punctuated by the *fort-da* between these two mothers. Like the title itself, *Rue Ordener, rue Labat*, the story of these mothers moves back and forth from one mother, one life, to another, each time across an unfathomable abyss, the rue Marcadet, which marks the narrative with so many interruptions or caesuras between one section and the next. Rue Ordener/rue Labat: even though the book moves from the father, the fountain pen of the father, the instrument with which Sarah Kofman will make a living and a name for herself, to the death of the adopted mother, Mémé, it leaves us where we began, in a place of alternation and repetition. Between the fortune-teller who tells of seeing her father surrounded by flames, all her problems with damned food, the double bind of eating and not eating, are the numerous separations from these two mothers, a constant ambivalence between a good mother and a bad, an insufferable transformation of one into the other, of the good breast into the bad.[18]

Nietzsche's Little Brother

But what happens when there is not only more than one mommy, more than one daddy, but more than one me—a sibling rivalry so intense that the sibling's death entails one's own? Sarah Kofman wrote autobiographical texts with a deceptive, cunning simplicity, knowing that the *autos* of autobiography is from the very beginning divided and multiplied, all autobiography a kind of retrospective illusion. We know that she knew this because in *Explosion I* and *Explosion II*, readings of Nietzsche's *Ecce Homo*, and in *Autobiogriffures*, a reading of E. T. A. Hoffmann's *The Cat Murr*, Sarah Kofman shows herself to be not only a clever reader of the ruses of autobiography, of the ways in which Hoffmann, for example, "deconstruct[s] the theological notion of author and book," the unity of biography or autobiography, by constructing a work full of citation and plagiarism, but also a cunning writer of her own autobiography through a discreet insinuation of herself into the autobiographies of others.[19] We see this most clearly in *Explosion I* and *Explosion II*, a brief reading of which will lead us back to the final pages of *Comment s'en sortir?*

Kofman calls Nietzsche's *Ecce Homo* the most "depersonalized autobiography that exists," "for its 'hero' has no easily recognizable father or mother, has no single figure, not even a single mask, a single Persona. In this sense, it is the autobiography of no one," the subject, the *autos*, always divided from itself and from the one who signs his work with the unique name Friedrich Nietzsche (Kofman 1992, 29). Because of this infinite division of the very self designated by "ecce homo" (Nietzsche, Christ, Dionysus, the Anti-Christ, Zarathustra, even Plato and Socrates), the autobiography becomes a mirror in which to read oneself, or rather, one's own "genealogical fantasy." Nietzsche's self-relation and self-reading provide Kofman with the opportunity to come into relationship with and read herself.

Hence, Kofman reads Nietzsche with an acute attentiveness to dates, as if watching for every sign of Nietzsche's attentiveness to dates would allow her, through the autobiography of another, to decipher the signs of her own life and destiny. First, then, the day, October 15, Nietzsche's birthday, a day that gives Nietzsche, as Kofman writes, "a particular affinity for Autumn, the season of fecundity and of the harvest"—the day, as we know, on which Kofman would take her own life in 1994.[20] Second, the year: Kofman draws attention to the way in which Nietzsche underscores the significance of *Ecce Homo*, described by Nietzsche as a gift given to himself on the occasion of his forty-fourth birthday (Kofman 1992, 11; see 146, 150, 354). Since Nietzsche is, as Kofman herself admits, a father figure for her, it is hard not to think here of Kofman's own father: Berek Kofman, born October 10, 1900, also in autumn therefore, in the year of both Nietzsche's death and the publication of Freud's monumental *Interpretation of Dreams*, and arrested in Paris in 1942, destined to perish at Auschwitz in his early forties. Now, were one to ask about the significance of this interest in dates in Kofman, we could find no better answer than Kofman's answer to the question of why there is such an interest in dates in Nietzsche. She writes, "[T]he quasi-obsessional importance put on birthdays and new years is related to the idea of mastering time and death" (1992, 155)—time and one's own death, I think we are to hear, but also, as we learn later, time and the other's death, time as the condition of all conversions, all transformations of good to bad. Dates, anniversaries: these too are but ways of making the intolerable tolerable, ways of keeping the brave day from slipping into hideous night. So important are these dates for Nietzsche and for Kofman that *Explosion I* ends with the enigma of a certain date in Nietzsche's life. We are somewhat prepared for this enigma earlier in the volume where Kofman speculates why Nietzsche, in 1879, and so at the age of thirty-five, rounded off his age to thirty-six at a crucial moment in his writing in order that the age at which his morbidity began might coincide with the date of his father's death. Kofman refers here to Nietzsche's "phantasmatic fiction" or "genealogical fantasy [généalogie fantastique]"—the same phrase used to describe Socrates-Diotima's myth of Eros in the *Symposium* (Kofman 1992, 170, 189).

Yet this particular manifestation of the will to fiction is less telling for Kofman than another, far more discreet and more repressed displacement of dates. Kofman ends volume 1 by referring to a "traumatic" event that had occurred to Nietzsche, according to him, when he was seven years old—an event that was decisive for his "wisdom" and his "life." Triggered by a phrase from *Ecce Homo*, from a section entitled "Why I Am So Wise," where Nietzsche writes, "Absurdly early, at the age of seven, I already knew that no human word could reach me," Kofman goes in search of the event at the origin of this enigmatic pronouncement. Like a good analyst, she reads these signs at face value in order to understand the mask behind the mask. She wonders how Nietzsche could have such a clear recollection of the age at which this event occurs, and whether this feigned loss of the ability to be wounded, this feigned insensitivity or invulnerability, does not correspond to a traumatic event that wounded and still wounds a very sensitive and vulnerable Nietzsche. Kofman asks, "The *pathos of distance*, symptom of his nobility, is this not the consequence of an intolerable childhood experience?" (1992, 383)—an experience or event that would have been not simply lost but repressed, an experience of which Nietzsche gives or retains but a date, "at the age of seven"? "Unless," speculates Kofman, "Nietzsche has chosen to place this decisive event at the age of seven because this number already had for him a fateful and magical connotation" (383). For Kofman recalls that in a letter written to his aunts when he was twenty-five Nietzsche underscores the importance of the seventh, fourteenth, and twenty-first years of life, since every seven years man, like a serpent, symbol of life and of its metamorphoses, takes on a new body, renews his life, rises, we could say, from his own ashes. The number seven will have thus always been fateful for Nietzsche, the very number of his fate. The age of reason for Christians, seven would perhaps be the age Nietzsche chose to signify his break with a Christian vision of the world and his embracing of a philosophy of the *amor fati*. Kofman ends *Explosion I*—or rather, to use her word, "suspends" it—with this enigma of a traumatic event in Nietzsche's life, "the enigma of the event whose traumatic character Nietzsche refused and that, come to the age of seven, was decisive for his destiny, his 'life' and his 'wisdom': that of the *Amor fati* that alone allowed him to become master of that from which he had the greatest need to preserve himself, master of ressentiment" (1992, 386). But what was this event, this traumatic wound from which Nietzsche would have constructed an entire philosophy in order to survive, an entire philosophy to make the intolerable tolerable? If one opens *Explosion II* expecting a quick resolution of the enigma Kofman develops at the end of *Explosion I*, one will be quickly and, then, for the time of some 380 pages, disappointed. It is only in the "conclusion" to *Explosion II: Les enfants de Nietzsche*, that Kofman really returns to the question with which she ended the first volume. She begins the conclusion: "But will we have really understood Nietzsche?" (1993c, 371). To answer this, to begin to answer this, we must first recognize the role that fiction always plays in reading the work of another, so that it is always less a question of understanding the other than of reading oneself, projecting upon, and interpreting the other, while reading oneself always between the lines. Kofman thus begins her conclusion by letting us in on this secret, letting the veil of commentary drop. She writes,

> [T]hroughout this work, which has followed him step by step, we will have, in any case, loved him: we will have been symbiotically united to him to the point of being confused with him; we will have been constantly fecundated by him, all the while trying ourselves, in some small way, to fecundate him.
>
> Could I have written about Nietzsche and his children with any justice, doing them justice, without myself becoming a child of Nietzsche? A child who, after having spent so many hours of her "life" so close to her "mother," finds herself forced, in the end, to cut the umbilical cord so as to become what she is?
>
> So as perhaps to write her own autobiography. (1993c, 371)

Kofman suggests that by following Nietzsche through this strange autobiography called *Ecce Homo* she is herself writing an autobiography of her own. She says in this same spirit that what Wagner and Schopenhauer were to Nietzsche, Freud and Nietzsche are to her—father figures, or, rather, mother figures—and she emphasizes how she always reads Freud and Nietzsche together, never letting one get the upper hand on the other. She ends the conclusion by making five points in reference to questions left open or in need of clarification in *Explosion I*. The fifth and final clarification concerns the number seven. Kofman recalls Nietzsche's interest in the number seven, its relation to the cult of Apollo—Apollo being the god of the veil (*Schleier*), the one who sifts and puts through a sieve the intolerable Dionysian "real" in order to let only what is tolerable come to light. She then remarks: "[T]o sift, filter, pass through a sieve, to censure—that is what is meant in German by the word *sieben*" (1993c, 381). Apollo, god of veils, is thus the god of both the number seven, *sieben*, and god of the censure, the censure and sieve of the Dionysian real (278, 380–84).

Sieben: this is another aporetic word for which the translator usually uses a good sieve to separate one meaning from the other, an aporetic word that Kofman now wants to restore to its full ambivalence. Reading Nietzsche as Freud might have done, Kofman suggests in light of Nietzsche's words on Dionysus and the number seven that the figure was chosen because of its "fateful and apocalyptic character" and because it "covers and counter-invests another censured figure, that of the real date at which the enigmatically traumatizing 'event' took place" (382). Hence a traumatic, Dionysian event occurs that is then censured, *sieben*, by Nietzsche, so that the only remaining trace is the enigmatic passage from *Ecce Homo* entitled "Why I Am So Wise," the only trace of the censuring work of *sieben*, and so of the traumatic event, the number *sieben*. Kofman's suggestion is that the traumatic, intolerable event, the unique, unincorporable event, has been passed through a sieve, transformed in order to make it past the censure, shrouded by the mask of seven so as to become, we might speculate, part of history or part of a series that begins 7, 14, 21, 28, 35, 42, and so on.

In the final paragraphs of *Explosion II*, Kofman lifts the veil and springs her hypothesis about the event, speculating that it just might have been the death of Nietzsche's younger brother Joseph, who died in February 1850, at the age of two, just months after the death of his father in July 1849, when Nietzsche was only five and a half. Kofman speculates that this may be the reason why this brother and his death are never mentioned in the autobiography *Ecce Homo*: this death would have been doubly intolerable, and so doubly in need of "censure," insofar as it would have corresponded, if we are to believe a dream that Nietzsche would have had just a few days before the death of Joseph, to a death wish: in this dream, Nietzsche sees his dead father coming to carry away his little brother. In order to tolerate this intolerable death and this even more intolerable death wish, "what was required was an entire censuring operation and the elaboration, very early, 'absurdly early,' of a wisdom, that of the *Amor fati*." Kofman concludes *Explosion II* by saying, "A simple hypothesis, a simple dream, on our part? Maybe. One can continue to dream by thinking that the existence of this little brother [ce frère cadet], the 'rival' against whom he directed a death wish . . . would have prevented him from becoming for his mother and in his own eyes an exceptional being, that this brother would have been the necessary second genius who would have kept him from 'madness'" (1993c, 384).

La ru(s)e Mar-cadet

So ends Kofman's truly extraordinary *Explosion* volumes—with an enigmatic reference to a traumatic event, enigmatic in Nietzsche, as Kofman shows, but also enigmatic for the importance Kofman attributes to it. Returning to the family scene of *Comment s'en sortir?* such a reference surely echoes what Kofman described as the interdependence of rival brothers like the sophist and the philosopher, of whom she said, I recall, that "the death of one signs the other's death warrant." But because she lets the veil drop and suggests that she has projected more than just a bit of herself into these volumes, we are licensed to ask, I think, about other reasons for this story of Nietzsche's brother, this *frère cadet* who died at the age of two. Why does Kofman place such significance on this family scene, and on this play of dates?

In Kofman's work, there is one date precisely given in a couple of places, one date emblazoned, so to speak, on her corpus: July 16, 1942—the date (as she puts it in the "Nightmare" attached to *Comment s'en sortir?*) that her father was "picked up" and sent off to die at Auschwitz. Born on September 14, 1934, Sarah would have been seven years old when this event, this traumatic event, occurred. It was on this day that the Kofman family of eight was reduced to seven, to the mother and her six children; and it would be from about this time forward that Sarah would begin struggling even more desperately, in the absence of her father, for the attention of her mother, or mothers, including the one who not only nourished and protected her but who frightened and threatened her with the specter of Maredewitch. In *Rue Ordener, rue Labat* Kofman introduces the figure of the old sorceress Maredewitch, so central to the closing pages of *Comment s'en sortir?*, by means of the mother (the ambivalent mother, the natural mother), who threatens Sarah and keeps her in line with dolls, lifelike dolls, doubles, and the threat that "Maredewitch" will come and get her if she does not behave. In her own analysis of the dream recounted in the final pages of *Comment s'en sortir?* Kofman almost immediately associates the menacing figure in her dream with Maredewitch, as she reflects upon and analyzes the ambivalent, aporetic syllable *mar*, which is inscribed even in the title of the section, "Cauche*mar*," "Night*mare*" (emphasis mine).[21] The dream is recounted in just a couple of lines:

> I am in a room from my childhood, with my mother, my brothers and sisters, at night. A bird enters, a kind of bat with a human head, pronouncing in a loud voice: Woe unto you! Woe unto you!
>
> My mother and I, terrorized, run away. We are in tears in the rue Marcadet; we know we are in great danger and fear death. I awaken very anxious.[22]

Between the rue Ordener and the rue Labat, Kofman tells us, there is the rue Marcadet—less a *rue* than a *chemin*, we could say, not a *hodos* for which a method could be designed to traverse it, but a *poros*, a path that must be engaged and traversed each time for the first time. La rue *Mar*-cadet: *mar*, syllable of malediction and misfortune in Old French, preserved, for Sarah, in her mother's invocation of the old sorceress Maredewitch; *mar*, just a vowel away from the *mer*, the ocean, the aporetic space par excellence for the Greeks and the best image for Plato, Kofman claims, of the sophistic aporia, *mer* or else its homonym *mère*, mother, or *mères*, mothers. *Mar*, *mer*, *mère*, *mères*—one can almost hear a young girl crying, *j'en ai marre*—I can't take it, it's intolerable, but then also *je me marre*, I'm laughing at it all. *Mar*, *mer*, *mère*, we are not even far from running into *mur*, not quite the *mur* of the fire wall but the murmuring Cat Murr, author of Hoffman's—so close to Kofman's—autobiography.[23] *Mar*, *mer*, *mur*: Kofman encourages this kind of vertiginous jubilation in the semiotic, this obsessive attentiveness to a syllable, through her own analysis of this oneiric sequence. Is it a coincidence, we thus might ask, that the syllable that haunts the final pages of *Comment s'en sortir?* is to be found in its very first word: "Mar-cel Detienne. . . ." Is this another ruse of the Promethean Kofman, hiding the *mar*, related to the Sanskrit for murder (as she herself reminds us)—behind this seemingly straightforward academic gesture?[24] I wouldn't put it past her.

Yet so much emphasis does she place on this syllable *mar* in *Marcadet* that we have to wonder—Sarah Kofman would encourage us to wonder—whether something intolerable is not being avoided in the other part of the word, *cadet*, meaning little brother, the word she introduced so dramatically (this "younger brother, this *frère cadet*, this rival") in the *very last* sentence of *Explosion II*. One has to wonder. For it just so happens that, like Nietzsche, Sarah Kofman too had a little two-year-old brother, a cadet, when she lost her father. Her little brother, named Isaac, had just turned two on July 14, that is, on 7.14.42, just two days before the arrest of her father. While I do not know—while I will never know—whether the word "cadet" conceals a similar kind of sibling rivalry as that which Kofman detects in Nietzsche, what we do know, from Kofman's own words, is that her brother's birth is in some way related to her father's death, for if Isaac had been less than two years old Sarah's father would not have been arrested, there being a rule that fathers of children under two not be deported. Moreover, the dream itself is suggestive of just such a rivalry. It begins, "I am in a room from my childhood, with my mother, my brothers and sisters," but when the threatening bird of misfortune arrives it is only she and her mother who flee, Sarah with her mother ("My mother and I, terrorized, run away"). Is this too a wish fulfillment? A death wish against or sacrifice of not just one sibling named Isaac but all five, all of them who, in the absence of her father, would now claim the attention of her mother? Just as, on Kofman's reading, the young Joseph would have claimed the attention of his mother and prevented Nietzsche from becoming the exceptional being he wished to become in her eyes? Mar-cadet, the accursed *cadet, dont on a marre, dont on se marre* (for "Isaac" also means "laughter"), whose sacrifice might reassure a frightened seven-year-old girl named Sarah that *ma mère maman mémé, mes mères m'aimaient*, that her mother, her mothers, loved her and only her? Murder, then, not on the rue Morgue but on the rue Marcadet? "A simple hypothesis, a simple dream, on our part? Maybe." What is certain is that Sarah Kofman knew that behind every family scene there is the intolerable, behind every form of remembrance an essential forgetting, behind the mask of every Promethean tragedy an Epimethean comedy. She knew better than most, and that is why we must remember her, that everything that goes down in history is destined to go down in flames.

March 14, 1987: A Memory?

I had wished to add as a sort of appendix to this essay a memory, an anecdote, an autobiographical story of my own about Sarah Kofman and fire—one that I have been telling myself and others for years now. But I now have reason to suspect that many of the "facts" of this anecdote are the result of what I might call a "genealogical fantasy" of my own. For what I had wished to relate were the facts surrounding a question I remember (or think I remember) Sarah Kofman asking Jacques Derrida in 1987, a question about spirit, fire, and ashes—in so many ways a perfectly Promethean question. Yet I have been unable to find a single shred of corroboration for my story, and so offer it here only as a testament to the anecdote I would like to have told and the memory I would like to have had.

It was March 14, 1987, and I was attending the final day of a conference on Heidegger at the Collège international de philosophie in Paris. The amphitheater was packed for the final keynote lecture by Jacques Derrida, and

I found myself toward the back of the room—not far, or so I thought, from Sarah Kofman, whom I had never before seen in person and would never see again. Derrida spoke for over three hours, reading the quasi totality of what would become *Of Spirit*. No one left, as I recall, and scarcely anyone moved, everyone knowing from the outset that we were not simply listening to a lecture but witnessing an event. I remember, and this much has at least has been confirmed by a copy of a letter I sent the next day to a friend in the United States, being profoundly moved—indeed, "stupefied"—by the lecture, which ended famously with the dramatic conversation between Heidegger and an imaginary theologian about the theological nature of Heidegger's writing.

When the lecture was over and the applause had died down, I recall Sarah Kofman asking the first question. She began by speaking of a painting by Max Ernst, a painting of 1935, she said, entitled *Fire and Ashes*, and then asked whether what Derrida was doing with Heidegger's work of the 1930s might not resemble or might have even taken inspiration from this painting. I remember, or I think I remember, saying to myself that while such a question did not address the lecture directly, and so could not possibly elicit much of a response from Derrida, it had somehow, in a mysterious way, penetrated to very heart of the matter. Though in some ways discontinuous with Derrida's lecture in both style and subject, it was, I thought, the perfect response—the perfect appendix—to it, a question that reverberated back upon the entire three-hour lecture I had just heard.

Haunted for years by that lecture and that question, I decided a couple of years ago to consult the audio archives of the Collège international de philosophie in order to take down Sarah Kofman's question verbatim and so add further detail to my anecdote. The tape containing Derrida's lecture had not been rewound, perhaps not even—as I would like to think—since it had been recorded in 1987; in any case, I began at the end, at what was labeled on the tape "part 2" of Derrida's lecture. Stopping not far into the question and answer period, working backward, I heard a female voice—Sarah Kofman's?—asking about Heraclitus and Nietzsche's eternal return in relation to Derrida's talk. Then, rewinding more, I came to several other questions, and then, letting the tape rewind for several seconds, to the final pages of Derrida's talk. Wanting at once to rekindle the emotion of hearing those pages for the first time and defer the pleasure of hearing Kofman's question, I listened again to the conversation between Heidegger and that imaginary theologian, I heard the applause, and, then, a sort of rustling sound, followed a couple of seconds later by Derrida responding to a question that had obviously not been picked up by the tape, a question, I thought I could make out from Derrida's response, about Georg Trakl and Heidegger. I let the tape continue and, to my utter dismay, I did not hear the question by Kofman I had been expecting: no *Fire and Ashes*, no 1935, none of the facts I needed for my anecdote. I rewound the tape to listen again, and, not surprisingly, I got the same results.

Quickly, reason came to cover over the confusion and form a hypothesis: just after Derrida's talk, the tape recorder was turned off, and because the microphone that would later be passed around the audience was not yet working, the recorder was not turned on again until Derrida's response to the second question—which came, as I remembered, from my colleague David Krell—a question about Trakl and the relationship between the brother and sister in his poetry. But I now have reasons to doubt this hypothesis: first, neither Derrida nor David Krell recall what questions were asked after the lecture, the latter being fairly certain that he did not ask a question that evening, not on Trakl and not on anything else. But also, and most disturbingly, I have been unable, despite numerous attempts, to find any painting by Max Ernst entitled *Fire and Ashes*. I say *Fire and Ashes* here because that is what it has been in my anecdote, even though Kofman would have said *Feu et cendres*, so close to Derrida's title *Feu la cendre*, published three years before, that I have begun to wonder whether I have not myself fabricated this title, or perhaps conflated it with Kofman's evocation, in homage to Blanchot, of an "écriture de cendres," a phrase that appeared in *Paroles souffoquées* in that very same year, 1987.

Though there are many connections with the work of Max Ernst, whose book of prints from 1934, *A Week of Kindness: Or, The Seven Deadly Elements*, has, as one of the elements, fire, though Ernst was clearly influenced by Kofman's two great influences, Freud and Nietzsche, though other paintings from 1935, like the *Petrified City* or the *Entire City*, or the *Fireside Angel* of 1937, suggest something to me of what I think I heard that night in 1987, I have found no trace of a painting entitled *Fire and Ashes*.[25] Perhaps Kofman herself was wrong about the title, or the date, or perhaps even the artist, inventing or transforming them, taming the fire, censoring and sifting in earnest to come up with another multiple of seven to get thirty-five.

The enigma remains to this day. The archive exists and yet Sarah Kofman's question would seem to have gone up in flames. Perhaps it is she later on asking about Heraclitus and the eternal return, but I am not certain. A single disruption—of the archive? of memory?—has been enough to put so much of the archive and my memory into doubt. Sarah Kofman's questioning voice has been lost. Yet rather than simply lament its loss or else resign myself to it, I would prefer, like Sarah Kofman, I think, to embrace it for a time like an *amor fati*.[26] To forget this loss and the lessons of it would be to forget Sarah Kofman and all that she has given and taught us; it would be to give in (too soon) to the conflagration that is destined to consume us all. To forget, to allow ourselves to forget—that is what is intolerable, especially when the intolerable is what must not be forgotten.

Notes

Unless otherwise indicated, all translations of Kofman's texts are the author's.

1. The quote continues "for not even the . . . kindly Prometheus escaped his heavy anger, but of necessity strong bands confined him, although he knew many a wile" (Hesiod 1943, 613–16).

2. This paper was first delivered at a conference on Sarah Kofman at DePaul University on October 12, 2001, just one month after September 11, 2001, as the ruins of the World Trade Center were, quite literally, still smoldering.

3. She writes: "From the pre-Socratics to Plato and beyond, Sarah Kofman trained generations of students in Paris in close and judicious reading of philosophical texts, and her first disciples were, as Socrates was the first to show [in action], her students" (Proust 1997, 8).

4. Most of *Comment s'en sortir?* has been translated by David Macey in Kofman 1988a, 7–44. The text opens and closes with a quote from Blanchot's *The Madness of the Day*, trans. Lydia Davis (Barrytown, NY: Station Hill Press, 1981), 7.

5. I note in passing that one of the plates of this Ernst book of 1929 is entitled, precisely, *Prometheus*.

6. See Derrida 1995, 88–127. For an analysis of the "and yet," see my "Given Time for a Detour," in *Taking on the Tradition: Jacques Derrida and the Legacies of Deconstruction* (Stanford, CA: Stanford University Press, 2003), 22–36.

7. In a context where other notables in France, such as Lacan, Irigaray, and Foucault, have already given influential readings of this same dialogue, Sarah Kofman's ruse is here a form of contestation. By questioning the paternal authority and agency of the father figure in Plato's myth of Eros, Kofman contests the authority of the readings of Plato that have preceded her. There were always, for Kofman, more than one father, and more than one mother, and since each can wear several masks, the proliferation of personae is nearly endless. See, for example, Lacan 1977, 322–23.

8. She begins, therefore, like Socrates, who, in a surprising number of dialogues, asks after or comments on the parents or kin of his philosophical interlocutors, while showing little to no interest in other details of their lives.

9. Like Zeus, the philosopher is "forced to swallow the *metis* of the sophists in order to use it against them and so as not to be dispossessed of this mastery" (Kofman 1988a, 16).

10. "Je ne suis ni ignorant ni savant" [I am neither ignorant nor knowing]: Blanchot's narrator is likened by Kofman in many of her books to Eros or to Socrates or else, in *Smothered Words*, to Oedipus (see 1998b, 77 n. 15).

11. In *Conversions*, Kofman speaks of the convertibility of opposites into one another, distinguishing the condition for this convertibility, a kind of "structural ambivalence," from any kind of mere "ambiguity" (1987a, 70).

12. See Kofman 1988a, 21–22 for Kofman's reading of the role aporia plays in the myth of the cave in the *Republic*. The hierarchy established between two types of

aporia is consistent with all the Platonic hierarchies, which privilege the intelligible at the expense of the sensible, the above over the below, light over darkness, male over female. It introduces a decisive division between sophistical aporia and philosophical aporia, and only the uneducated, according to Plato, can confuse the two.

13. In *The Childhood of Art* (1988b) Kofman follows Freud in reading works of art not as the creation of a father-genius-god but as a symptom of what has been repressed, of forces that go beyond those of the artist. Through a kind of "deconstruction" of the idealization of the artist into a great man or genius, into a father, the work of art is read no longer as the brainchild of its creator, but as a symptom of some repressed pleasure, fantasy, or, indeed, trauma.

14. Kofman 1988b, 170. Freud's substitution of procreation for creation "unmasks a conception of paternity tainted by the theological model which is itself the idealized projection of it." In his analysis of Leonardo da Vinci, Freud "puts an end," according to Kofman, "to the theological conception of art" and its expression of "infantile wishes" by putting "an end to the illusion that the parents of each one of us wanted us for ourselves, that we are chosen beings." Kofman concludes that "the entire traditional ideology of art was intended to repress the absence of foundation of all life" (170).

15. On this pharmaceutical function of beauty in art, see Kofman 1985b, 76.

16. Kofman argues that Plato in the *Sophist* puts "the 'subtle' friends of ideas and the 'vulgar' ones of the sensible realm back to back, in order to show that they both attempt to conceal in a fictitious way that part of reality which is *intolerable* to them" (1987b, 42; my emphasis). She later claims in this same essay that philosophers create fictions of logic and concepts "aimed at falsifying the world of becoming (such as Heraclitus's genius envisioned it) by restraining it within human, too human dimensions, in order to make the *intolerable, tolerable*: change, contradictions, death, the endless conflict of opposing forces. Their logic and their concepts allow them to perceive 'some solid ground in the sea of becoming'" (47; my emphasis).

17. In *Explosion I* Kofman speaks of Nietzsche, the last disciple of Dionysus, as wearing in *Twilight of the Idols* and *Ecce Homo* a luminous Apollinian mask designed to "bear the unbearable" and "prepare the reader to tolerate the intolerable" (1992, 104).

18. See the chapter of *Explosion I* entitled "Wagner's good breast" (Kofman 1992, 337–46).

19. See Kofman 1984a 17, 116. According to Kofman, Hoffmann's text "deconstructs" the unity of biography or autobiography.

20. Here is another of the many references to Nietzsche and birthdays in the *Explosion* volumes: "Born on October 15, Nietzsche feels a particular affinity for Autumn, the season of fecundity and of the harvest" (Kofman 1992, 146).

21. This "autobiographical" reading of Sarah Kofman's work is hardly antithetical to Kofman's work. Indeed, Kofman herself already begins this reading in *Rue Ordener, rue Labat* (1996) where she makes the connection between her own two mothers and her interest in Freud's reading of Leonardo da Vinci's two mothers, or

where she says that the dark room in which her mother would shut her up was not unrelated to her book *Camera Obscura.*

22. Kofman 1983a, 108–9; English translation by Frances Barkowski in Kofman 1986a, 12. For a superb analysis of this text in the context of a reading of Kofman and/as Antigone, and of the breakdown or caesura of the speculative in the syllable *mar*, see Tina Chanter, "Tragic Dislocations: Antigone's Modern Theatrics," *Difference* 10, No. 1 (1998): 85–87.

23. Unless "Kofman" is a combination of "Kafka" and "Hoffmann"; see Kofman 1986a, 9–10.

24. "The syllable *mar*, which Kofman tracks through misery and grief, is from the Sanskrit verb 'murder'" (Kofman 1986a, 7). She interprets the Maredewitch in the dream as the Gestapo commander who came to take them from their home on the rue Ordener.

25. Ernst 1976; the third element is fire.

26. Kofman writes of the *amor fati* at the end of *Explosion I*: "[T]his formula . . . affirms that man is great enough not simply to accept, like the Stoics, whatever happens as it happens, to put up with the inevitable in a sort of passive submission to a destiny before which we are powerless; even less does it imply dissimulating this ineluctablity, tolerating the intolerable by fictionalizing a phantasmatic and illusory neo-reality like a deceptive metaphysical or religous idealism does but to love this ineluctability. *Amor fati* is a true love because it is not resigned; it does not give itself over to a pseudo divine will but wants and affirms the totality of what is, what was, and what will be, for all time. . . . The *Amor fati* is an 'unlimited Amen' (1992, 384).

CHAPTER 5

Le mépris des anti-sémites: Kofman's Nietzsche and Nietzsche's Jews

ALAN D. SCHRIFT

> How does it happen that the human subject makes himself into an object of possible knowledge, through what forms of rationality, through what historical necessities, and at what price? My question is this: How much does it cost the subject to be able to tell the truth about itself?
>
> —Michel Foucault, "How Much Does It Cost to Tell the Truth?"

Let me begin with an acknowledgment and a confession. First the acknowledgment: when Sarah Kofman chose to end her life—on October 15, 1994, the 150th anniversary of the day Friedrich Nietzsche's life began—she had as thorough a familiarity with and command over Nietzsche's writings as anyone I have met. This should be kept in mind as I make the following remarks because, if I choose to challenge Kofman's interpretation of Nietzsche's relation to the Jews, this challenge speaks more to *why* Kofman chose to interpret Nietzsche on this issue as she did than to my presumption to correct a misinterpretation she might have made. In other words, my remarks question Kofman's *desire* rather than her knowledge; they question her desire to read Nietzsche as she did rather than question any interpretative errors she might have made in this reading.

And now the confession: this paper has a very personal origin, one that dates to the first time I met Sarah Kofman. That meeting took place in the spring of 1994 at the Nietzsche Society meeting at the University of Swansea organized by Duncan Large in honor of the sesquicentennial of Nietzsche's birth. Sarah was the keynote speaker, and she read a shortened version of what turned out to be her last published work on Nietzsche, entitled *Le mépris des Juifs: Nietzsche, les Juifs, l'antisémitisme* (Contempt for the Jews: Nietzsche, the

Jews, Anti-Semitism) (1994b). For those of you who did know Sarah, you know that she could be, let us say, difficult. But she could also be very sweet, and very generous. For reasons that I will never fully understand, she and I hit it off quite well in Swansea. I was at the time not as good as I should have been with spoken French, and though Sarah was not generally comfortable speaking English, she was quite willing to converse with me in English that weekend. During our conversations in Swansea, she talked about her autobiography, *Rue Ordener, rue Labat*, which at the time had recently appeared to favorable reviews in Paris. In that context, she confided to my wife and I that she thought I bore a resemblance to her father. When someone who knows the texts of Freud as well as Kofman does makes such a comment, the temptation to bring in the machinery of psychoanalytic decoding is difficult to resist, but fortunately I did resist, especially since it was not until some months later that I read her autobiography and learned the fate of her father at the hands of the Nazis in 1942.[1]

Before she left Swansea, Sarah gave me a copy of her book on Nietzsche and the Jews, and she invited me to visit her in Paris when I would be there the following summer. This I did, and that was to be the second and final time we met. We talked for several hours about all sorts of Nietzscheana, and it was in that context that I came to the conclusion that I was with someone whose knowledge of Nietzsche's works was unparalleled. During that visit, my resemblance to her father came up again. This time, however, I was shown a photograph of him, and my silence was even more pronounced than it was in response to her earlier comment because, while both this photograph and my resemblance to her father were obviously important to her, I could see absolutely no resemblance between her father and myself. What she saw I will never know, for we did not talk any further about her father, and her death made pursuing the issue impossible. The connection between us—between Sarah, her murdered father Baruch, and myself—is indelibly connected to that book that she gave me in Swansea, *Le mépris des Juifs: Nietzsche, les Juifs, l'antisémitisme*, and in its own way, this little book has had an impact on my own reading of Nietzsche greatly disproportionate to its size, for Kofman's book on the Jews demanded that I confront a question that I had for over twenty years avoided, a very personal question—namely, the question of what it means to read Nietzsche "as a Jew."

This question is interesting not least because it has been raised so rarely, a fact especially noteworthy in the contemporary context of Nietzsche's highly self-reflexive scholarly audience. A marked self-reflexivity is particularly apparent in recent readings of Nietzsche by feminists, for whom the question of what it means to read Nietzsche "as a woman" is de rigueur. It certainly warrants notice, then, that for all the problematic associations between Nietzsche and Nazism, there has never been a shortage of significant Jewish interpreters of Nietzsche. In addition to Kofman, we can also name his first important English-language commentators—Walter Kaufmann and Arthur Danto—as well as (restricting the list to authors of multiple volumes on Nietzsche) Jacques Derrida, Bernd Magnus, Alexander Nehamas, and Gary Shapiro.[2] Yet for all the important Jewish interpreters, this question of reading Nietzsche "as a Jew" rarely comes up. But it should, shouldn't it? It even came up for Nietzsche, didn't it? Didn't he note, not always with pleasure, that his "first" commentator, Georg Brandes, was a Jew? Are Nietzsche's supposedly anti-Semitic remarks any easier to pass over than his supposedly misogynistic remarks? I do not think they are. But then why do so many women who write on Nietzsche feel compelled to address comments like "You are going to woman? Do not forget the whip?" or "Everything about woman is a riddle, and everything about woman has one solution: that is pregnancy,"[3] while most of Nietzsche's Jewish readers pass over in relative silence remarks like this one, from *On the Genealogy of Morals* where he writes that in contrast to the Romans, "The *Jews* were the priestly nation of *ressentiment par excellence*"; or that, as he writes in *Beyond Good and Evil*, the significance of the Jewish people is that "with *them* begins the *slave revolt in morals*" or that, as he notes in *Human, All Too Human*, "perhaps the youthful stock-exchange Jew is the most repulsive invention of the entire human race."[4]

Of course, this is not to say that all of Nietzsche's Jewish readers pass over his remarks like these without noticing them. But it does seem odd that so many of Nietzsche's commentators, and some of the most important commentators, *are* in fact Jewish and, more significantly, they, or should I say *we*, are able to pass over remarks that would almost certainly cause offense were we, in almost any other context, to hear them spoken in our presence? Why don't Nietzsche's remarks bother me? Or do they? And did they bother Sarah Kofman? Was this perhaps *why*, after spending so many years working on Nietzsche's autobiographical *Ecce Homo*, she chose after publishing her childhood memoir *Rue Ordener, rue Labat* to return again to Nietzsche and address the question of his supposed "contempt for the Jews."

Reading *Le mépris des Juifs*, one cannot but be struck by the rigor of her defense of Nietzsche against the charge of anti-Semitism. In fact, it does not seem inappropriate to regard her account as nothing short of "miraculous" in the sense that Bataille gives to that term. You may recall that, in the third volume of *The Accursed Share*, Bataille recounts his coming to understand why tears of happiness welled up in his eyes when he told the story of his cousin's miraculous assignment to another ship hours before the naval vessel on which he had served was sunk with all hands lost. The miraculous quality, Bataille remarks, "is conveyed rather exactly by the expression: *impossible and yet there it is*" (1991, 206). It was something like this sense of the miraculous that I experienced when first reading Kofman's text: not only was Nietzsche *not* an anti-Semite but, according to Kofman, "the Jew who had become a great man—even more than the Renaissance man—could serve as a model for the '*Übermensch*' and bolster hope in the advent of that figure who until then had been purely 'ideal' and fictitious, with Zarathustra as his sole incarnation."[5] The true Sabbath, in whose advent Nietzsche takes delight, "will be a celebration not so much of the birth of a new Adam as the return of the Jew of the Biblical age, of the Jew who, at the peak of his power, was able to create in his own image and in the likeness of his prophets and of Moses a majestic, omnipotent, choleric and jealous God" (Kofman 1994b, 47–48). Kofman, who had so great a command over Nietzsche's texts, had come to these conclusions when reflecting on Nietzsche's supposed contempt for the Jews. Impossible, and yet there it is!

As an aside, I should here note that Kofman is not completely alone in coming to this conclusion, for another of Nietzsche's Jewish interpreters, Yirmiyahu Yovel, reaches a similar conclusion in his 1998 book *Dark Riddle: Hegel, Nietzsche, and the Jews*. There Yovel argues that the affirmation of the contemporary Diaspora Jews is central to Nietzsche's philosophical project. Just as Nietzsche appealed to the figure of Zarathustra—the inventor of morality—when he sought a figure to now initiate the overcoming of morality (see *Ecce Homo*, "Why I am a Destiny," sec. 3, in Nietzsche 1967), Yovel claims that insofar as the Jews gave birth to the scourge of European culture—that is, Christianity—Nietzsche concludes that the task must fall to the Jews to assist in curing Europe from this illness from which it has suffered for two millennia. As Yovel puts it, "The Jewish issue is linked to two critical events in Nietzsche's narrative of European history: the rise of Christian decadence . . . and the expected overcoming of this decadence in post-Christian Europe. Both the ancient slave revolution in morality and the curative revaluation of values expected in the future are crucial moments in Nietzsche's philosophical project, and both have the Jews playing a central role. The Jews who corrupted culture in the guise of (proto-Christian) priests must now help redeem it as secularized post-Christian new Europeans" (1998, 180).

I must admit, however, that I am not completely persuaded, either by Yovel or by Kofman. Of course, Nietzsche was not the *reichsdeutsch* anti-Semite that his sister Elizabeth and others wanted him to be, and that too many readers on both sides of the Channel have thought him to be. But was he really such a great friend of the Jews? And is it really the case that in order for Nietzsche to become-Nietzsche, he had to become a Jew? For this is, after all, the ingenious conclusion to which Kofman's text leads, as she argues that ultimately Nietzsche becomes who and what he is by settling accounts—"cutting the umbilical cord"—once and for all, "with the Germany of the Reich, with his mother and his sister, and with the paternal substitutes who had been, among others, Wagner and Schopenhauer" (1994b, 76). To settle these accounts meant settling accounts with the anti-Semitism that was perhaps their central unifying feature. Kofman suggests this is the reason why Nietzsche identified himself in *Ecce Homo*, the text that exercised such fascination over her, with precisely those characteristics—being clever (*klug*) and wise (*weise*)—that the people in Lessing's *Nathan the Wise* attribute to the Jews. A fascinating hypothesis, and one that leads quite naturally to another: Is this why Nietzsche concluded that he is a destiny? Is his destinal status and world-historical significance the final act of his identification with the "Chosen People"?

But do we want to go this far? Do we really want to claim that Nietzsche's decision to revalue all values led him to "necessarily and systematically" affirm in the Jews precisely those features that he should have despised had his family's and his mentors' anti-Semitic teachings successfully been instilled in him? While one must agree with Kofman's judgment that one can make Nietzsche the father of National Socialism and its racism "only at the cost of an interpretive violence" (1994b, 73), there may nevertheless be more than a little textual blindness involved in attributing all of Nietzsche's hostility toward the Jews to his Wagnerian-Schopenhauerian youthful exuberance and the pernicious ideas of his family.

It is, therefore, particularly surprising to find Kofman noting, on the one hand, the plurality and complexity of Nietzsche's texts, while on the other hand accusing those who conclude that Nietzsche was an anti-Semite of "bad faith and a self-satisfied blindness to the text's *strict literality*" (75; emphasis added). What are we to make of this notion of "strict literality"? Is what it means to be an "anti-Semite" so clear and unambiguous? And does *not* being anti-Semitic mean that one is necessarily, ipso facto, pro-Semitic or philo-Semitic? It might be worthwhile here to introduce a distinction, made much of by Hannah Arendt in *The Origins of Totalitarianism*, between being anti-Semitic and being anti-Jewish, and note that while Nietzsche is most definitely *not* anti-Semitic, his judgments concerning the worth of Jewish values remains ambivalent at best.[6] If Nietzsche's admiration of certain aspects of Jewish values and value judgments is conjoined with deep suspicion and dissatisfaction with other aspects of Jewish valuation, what effect should this have on our own judgments concerning Nietzsche's "strict literality" on "the Jewish question"?

Let me be clear here about the point of these questions. It is absolutely evident that Kofman was correct to point out that Nietzsche was a constant critic of both the politics of German nationalism and the politics of anti-Semitism; but it is no less evident that Nietzsche's rhetorical "excesses" can and do leave him open to be interpreted in a wide variety of ways. And insofar as Nietzsche sanctions creative interpretation as an act of affirmative will to power, he can perhaps be held accountable—or at least more accountable than Kofman seemed to wish—for accommodating those interpretations that allowed some of his more rhetorically charged and superficially anti-Jewish remarks to eclipse his consistent and firm renunciation of the politics of anti-Semitism.[7]

This point has already been made by Jacques Derrida, among others, in response to the Nazi appropriation of Nietzsche. In particular, one of the points that emerges in the context of Derrida's reading in "Otobiographies" of Nietzsche's 1872 text *On the Future of Our Educational Institutions* is that Nietzsche wrote some things that do in fact lend themselves to the sort of use made of his works by the Nazis. As Derrida notes, while it may be contrary to the intention of those he derisively refers to as the "shareholders in the huge 'Nietzsche Corporation,' . . . it cannot be entirely fortuitous that the discourse bearing his name in society, in accordance with civil laws and editorial norms, has served as a legitimating reference for ideologues. There is nothing absolutely contingent about the fact that the only political regimen to have *effectively* brandished his name as a major and official banner was Nazi" (1985, 30–31). Which is to say, it is not just the result of an unfortunate coincidence or Nietzsche's bad luck that his works, rather than the works of Kant or Leibniz, became linked as they did with National Socialism.

Does this make Nietzsche a Nazi? Of course not. It does, however, say something about his texts and the risks that writers run when they allow their works to enter the sphere of public discourse—namely, when they make their writings public, they sanction de facto their work being appropriated and grafted onto other contexts. These risks, however, become extreme when a writer chooses to write with the hyperbolic rhetoric that one finds in Nietzsche, and perhaps this explains why Nietzsche's words have been well-received by extremists on the left and the right almost since his texts first appeared.[8]

No one knew this better than Sarah Kofman, whose brilliant first book on Nietzsche, *Nietzsche et la métaphore* (1972), did as much as any single text to draw attention to the *philosophical* significance of Nietzsche's rhetorical skills.[9] In that book, in contradistinction to an interpretive strategy like that of Heidegger, which strives to isolate what is "essential" in Nietzsche's thought, Kofman argued that we should avoid speaking of what Nietzsche's metaphors "really mean" or what his images "essentially" represent in favor of suggesting that we can reread Nietzsche's text from the perspective of its strategic metaphorical transformations. If Nietzsche had an "essential thought" to express, Kofman implied, he would have chosen a style of philosophical discourse more conducive to the task of its unambiguous expression. Unlike Descartes, for example, whose method sought the metaphysical roots out of which the tree of philosophical truth grows, Kofman saw Nietzsche providing us with an *arbre fantastique*, one that would be "the best paradigm of the new philosopher, who affirms life in all its forms, multiplying and displacing his perspectives without referring to any absolute and definitive center" (1993b, 111; 1972, 162). Rather than seeking the sturdy roots of the Cartesian tree so as to legitimate its fruits, Nietzsche prefers to play among the branches of this fantastic tree, tasting all the varied fruits that it brings forth. This fantastic tree, concludes Kofman, is life itself, and it has many offshoots that bear many different kinds of fruit, some ripe and others rotten.

By cultivating such a fantastic tree, Kofman noted that Nietzsche ran the risk of being misunderstood. And, she argued, Nietzsche not only accepted this risk; he *willed* it (1993b, 112; 1972, 163), claiming being misunderstood as a title of honor (see Nietzsche 1974, sec. 371). His aphorisms, the fruit of his fantastic tree, are offered only to those who have the ears for them. His aristocratic style forsakes the goal of communicating with all in favor of communicating only with those few—the disciples of Dionysus—who know how his text should be read.[10] Only these readers will be able to follow Nietzsche's "dance with the pen," and they alone will be able to accept the invitation to dance that his aphorisms offer. These readers will elevate reading to the level of an art; they will recognize the aphorism as the "writing itself of the will to power," and "on every metaphor will ride to every truth."[11] *Nietzsche et la métaphore* concluded on this note, suggesting that the ability to dance among aphorisms is another of Nietzsche's principles of selection that distinguish those with noble instincts from the *profanum vulgus*.

While I applauded this conclusion when I first read her work, the times have changed and I suppose I have changed. In looking back on her conclusion today, I find myself uncomfortable with remarks from *Nietzsche et la métaphore* like this one: "[A]phoristic writing and metaphorical style distinguish men from one another and keep at a distance the common run, the 'democratic' plebs, those who are not clean" (Kofman 1993b, 117). For while I still remain committed to viewing Nietzsche's texts as multiple, capable of multiplying meanings in the hands of multiple readers, I have become more sensitive to the uses that can be made of some of these multiple meanings. Which is only to say, playing with the metaphor Kofman herself provided, that some of the fruit from Nietzsche's fantastic tree may be very rotten indeed. While left-leaning readers of Nietzsche have legitimately criticized those readings that make Nietzsche out to be a "simple" misogynist, or a straightforwardly anti-Semitic or anti-Enlightenment thinker, there remain problems with many of those readings that seek to "save" Nietzsche from charges of misogyny or anti-Semitism or to make him compatible with a leftist or left-leaning liberal-democratic politics. Rather than directly confront and take account of them, the price paid for the political packaging of Nietzsche as a champion of the left is often to choose to overlook as insignificant or momentary lapses Nietzsche's many crudely racist, sexist, or elitist remarks. With a writer whose prose is both as nuanced and as excessive as Nietzsche's, a certain amount of selective inattention may be unavoidable. But as philosophical and political centers are shifting to the right, which appears to be the case as we begin a new millennium, we overlook the less progressive of Nietzsche's remarks at our peril.[12]

Does this mean one should give up on Nietzsche? I don't think so. For there is reason still to be optimistic about the future of Nietzsche's legacy, especially insofar as the identity politics that has produced ethnic nationalisms in eastern Europe and Africa calls for a critical response in which the Nietzschean critiques of both identity and nationalism can be of value. In fact, the grounds for such a Nietzschean account might be located in one of his passages on the Jews that, surprisingly, Sarah Kofman did not cite in *Le mépris des Juifs*. In section 475 of *Human, All Too Human*, Nietzsche offers one of his most powerful indictments of nationalism. In the context of rejecting the artificial and perilous separation of Europe into distinct nations through the "production of *national* hostilities," Nietzsche suggests that it is not the interests of the many but the interests of a few—"certain princely dynasties and certain classes of business and society"—that "impel to this nationalism." It is precisely at this point that Nietzsche situates the origins of modern anti-Semitism: "[T]he entire problem of the Jews," he writes, "exists only in national states." He continues, in a passage that should refute definitively the simple-minded charge of straightforward anti-Semitism: "It is here that their energy and higher intelligence, their capital in will and spirit accumulated from generation to generation in a long school of suffering, must come to preponderate to a degree calculated to arouse envy and hatred, so that in almost every nation—and the more so the more nationalist a posture the nation is adopting—there is gaining ground the literary indecency of leading the Jews to the sacrificial slaughter as scapegoats for every possible public or private misfortune."[13] Whether Nietzsche himself may succumb at times to an identity politics at the level of culture or ethnicity that his philosophical critique of nationalism should have distanced him from is, of course, a matter worth addressing. But insofar as he here provides tools for a critique of national identity in favor of the "production of the strongest possible European mixed race," there is reason to look to his critique as a possible resource for criticizing a politics of ethnic or cultural identity as well.[14]

Similarly, the Nietzschean critique of dogmatism, grounded as it is on a perspectivist position that calls for multiplying points of view and avoiding fixed and rigid posturings, may be an important voice to heed in constructing a politics that can challenge the panoply of emerging fundamentalisms. At the same time, a thoroughgoing perspectivism can accommodate a notion of radical contingency that seems to be both theoretically desirable and pragmatically necessary at the present moment to many who—from the perspectives of feminism and women's studies, gender studies, queer theory, minoritarian studies, cultural studies, and, more generally, from any oppositional perspective—hope to move from theory to action. Which is only to say that seeing the world with more and different eyes may become a political necessity if one hopes to succeed, paraphrasing Marx's Eleventh Thesis on Feuerbach, in not simply interpreting the world, but changing it as well.[15]

With this in mind, I would like venture a few final thoughts on the question of Nietzsche and the Jews. My response to this question differs from Kofman's in that, ultimately, I do not find any great love in Nietzsche for the Jews. In several recent discussions of Nietzsche and the Jews or Judaism, it has become common to distinguish between three phases of Judaism, toward each of which Nietzsche adopts a different response. To cite one example, Yovel puts the point nicely: "[W]ithin historical Judaism, three stages are to be distinguished: Old Testament Judaism, whose 'grandeur' Nietzsche adored; the 'priestly' Judaism of the Second Temple, which he profoundly despised and condemned as the parent of Christian culture; and the post-Christian Judaism of Jews in the Diaspora and in modern times, whom he defended, admired, and saw as a healing ingredient in his 'new Europe'" (1988, 117).[16] While I agree that this distinction is to be found in Nietzsche's comments on the Jews, and while I think Kofman would be sympathetic to such a typology, I still am not convinced that Nietzsche's *anti*-anti-Semitism is an active affirmation of Semitism or Jews. Rather, it seems to me that Nietzsche provides a reactive negation of anti-Semitism that is often motivated by something other than an unequivocally positive appraisal of Jews or Judaism.

In other words, I think that while Nietzsche might respect the severity and grandeur of pre-prophetic Old Testament or First Temple Judaism and while he might admire certain Jewish individuals (Mendelssohn, Heine, Spinoza, perhaps even Jesus), he is for the most part content to *use* the Jews and Jewish identity for his own rhetorical purposes.[17] In that sense, I would agree with Kofman that Nietzsche champions the Jews in attacking the anti-Semitism of his sister Elizabeth, of Wagner, or of Schopenhauer. We see this most clearly in *Der Antichrist*, a text whose title, as many have noted, is perhaps better translated as *The Antichristian* than *The Antichrist*. But this text offers a good example, as well, of what I mean by Nietzsche's "using" of the Jews. There is little doubt that, as a text, *Der Antichrist* is a declaration of war on Christianity. And as a tactic within that war, Nietzsche uses the Christian disdain for the Jews as a weapon against Christianity itself, showing that what is most Christian can be genealogically traced back to Jewish roots. His affirmation of the Jews in *Der Antichrist* is thus rhetorically charged primarily to insult Christians rather than to affirm Jews. But to say that Nietzsche is anti-anti-Semitic or anti-Christian is not to say that he is pro-Semitic or pro-Jewish. It is therefore mistaken, I think, to conclude that Nietzsche's treatment of the Jews in *Der Antichrist* is in any way a genuine or authentic compliment:

Judaism remains at bottom little more than the decadent soil out of which sprang what Nietzsche regarded to be that most rotten and poisonous of fruit: Christianity.

But the case of *On the Genealogy of Morals* is perhaps even more problematic, for here one sees that for all of his admiration "in theory" for the Jews, so forcefully presented in Kofman's account, Nietzsche could quickly return to those anti-Semitic prejudices that Kofman and others want to attribute to his Wagnerian and Schopenhauerian youthful indiscretions. Thus, while Nietzsche may still be having his fun with his Christian and anti-Semitic readers by continually rubbing their noses in the fact that the roots of Christianity lie in Jewish soil, we should not lose sight of the fact that Nietzsche concludes the First Essay by framing the battle between noble and base values as the struggle between Rome and Judea, a struggle that resulted in the victory of the slave revolt in morality. For those who need help in reading the contemporary signs of this victory, Nietzsche offers the following remark: "Which of them has won *for the present*, Rome or Judea? But there can be no doubt: consider to whom one bows down in Rome itself today, as if they were the epitome of all the highest values—and not only in Rome but over almost half the earth, everywhere that man has become tame or desires to become tame: *three Jews*, as is known, and *one Jewess* (Jesus of Nazareth, the fisherman Peter, the rug weaver Paul, and the mother of the aforementioned Jesus, named Mary)."[18] As one follows the references to Jews in Nietzsche's texts, I want to argue that one finds a noticeable hostility in one text above all—namely, *On the Genealogy of Morals*. One critic has argued that the answer to the question of why this is the case might be located in Nietzsche's human, all too human psychology. Rudolph Binion, in *Frau Lou: Nietzsche's Wayward Disciple*, suggests that *On the Genealogy of Morals*, subtitled a "A Polemic [Eine Streitschrift]" is a polemical rejoinder not just to Paul Rée's *The Origin of the Moral Sensations*, but to Rée himself and the role he played in the relations between Nietzsche and Lou Salomé.[19] And if this is the case, might it be that, when all is said and done, Rée emerged for Nietzsche as little more than a Jew, whose Jewishness accounted for his less than noble behavior during the whole so-called Lou affair. This was, after all, the judgment of Rée made earlier by the "other woman" in Nietzsche's life, Cosima Wagner, who wrote in reaction to Nietzsche's defense of the Jews in *Human, All Too Human*, "Finally Israel intervened in the form of a Dr. Rée, very sleek, very cool, at the same time as being wrapped up in Nietzsche and dominated by him, though actually outwitting him—the relationship between Judea and Germany in miniature."[20]

If this hypothesis of transference has some plausibility, it would show Nietzsche, like all anti-Semites, to be guilty of essentializing in the most base and racist manner his former friend's ethnic identity into his very definition. That is to say, were this hypothesis an accurate reflection of Nietzsche's inner life, it would show him, perhaps at a moment of weakness, to be guilty of the paradigmatic *racist* gesture—*turning the multiplicity of an individual into a simple incarnation of a racial stereotype.*

But should we accept this rather crude psychological hypothesis that wants to analyze Nietzsche's criticism of Jews in *On the Genealogy of Morals* as a reaction-formative displacement of his hostility toward Paul Rée for sabotaging Nietzsche's advances toward Lou? Put so bluntly, it seems rather ridiculous; but while such a hypothesis most likely could not be proven, there is other evidence that supports it. This evidence, which like Binion's is circumstantial, I would locate in Nietzsche's drafts of letters from mid-July 1883 to Rée and to his brother George Rée, in which he accuses Paul Rée of having behaved "behind [his] back as a sneaking, slanderous, mendacious partner [als schleichender, verleumderischer, verlogener Gesell]" and suggests that he would "take great pleasure in giving [Rée] a lesson in practical morality with a few bullets."[21] Had Nietzsche really been guilty, as Binion suggests, of a sort of psychoanalytic transference from Rée's Jewishness to his criticisms of Jews in *On the Genealogy of Morals*, one might expect to find this tendency previewed in these almost hysterical letters of 1883, and unfortunately it is. For while there is no direct reference to Rée's being Jewish, the adjectives Nietzsche chooses to use here—*schleichender, verleumderischer, verlogener*—are not uncommon in the anti-Semitic rhetoric of the day. This certainly does not prove Binion's case, and even if Nietzsche had these anti-Semitic sentiments toward Rée personally, an explanatory leap is made in appealing to these sentiments to explain Nietzsche's treatment of the Jews in *On the Genealogy of Morals* that I am not comfortable making. I should hasten to add that it is not just a lack of comfort that prevents me from following Binion here, for my intuition is that if Nietzsche had internalized an anti-Semitic or anti-Jewish *ressentiment* toward Rée between 1883 and 1886, one might expect to find some negative reference or connotation to Rée's being Jewish in *Ecce Homo*; but here, on the contrary, Nietzsche's references to Rée as well as Lou in this text are even-tempered and positive, even as his criticisms of Germans, particularly his mother and sister, are not.[22]

This, of course, leaves open the question of why Nietzsche is so critical of the Jews in *On the Genealogy of Morals*, a question left open by Kofman's text as well. My suspicion, and it is only a suspicion, is that while he was never driven *primarily* by anti-Semitism, Nietzsche did not really care for Jews, and he certainly did not have many dealings with Jewish people. As a result, while he was consistently critical of the politics of anti-Semitism, he made use of Judaism as an analytic category when it suited him to do so. In his earliest works, under the influence of Wagner and Schopenhauer, although he distanced himself from their more overtly anti-Semitic political determinations, he largely accepted their judgments concerning the Jews.[23] During his middle period, when he was quite friendly with Paul Rée, among others, he wanted to sever his earlier personal commitments, and toward that end he actively extolled the virtues of Judaism and certain particular Jews. But when, at the end of his productive life, the time came to make war on Christianity, he used the Jews and Judaism as a weapon in this war. Thus, in *Der Antichrist*, where the battle involved direct assault on Christianity, Semitism made an attractive weapon by which to point out the life-negating attributes of Christianity and further the contrast between Jesus's life and Paul's (mis)interpretation of it. But in *On the Genealogy of Morals*, where the case against Christianity is made on "historical/genealogical" grounds, Judaism and the Jews stand not as a contrast but as the diseased origin out of which Christianity grew. Thus, as Sarah Kofman correctly points out, Nietzsche is neither inconsistent nor contradictory in this treatment of the Jews. Rather, like a *bricoleur*, he uses them as called for in furthering the ultimate goal of his argument.

This, I would argue, is a conclusion close to the one arrived at by Yovel that I discussed earlier. But unlike Yovel, who sees Nietzsche's unambivalent rejection of anti-Semitism conjoined with an equally unambivalent affirmation of contemporary Jews, I find no such pro-Jewish affirmation in Nietzsche's late works. And insofar as Nietzsche does *use* the Jews to further his own war against Christianity, this puts the Jewish reader of Nietzsche, like the woman reader of Nietzsche, in a sometimes very awkward and uncomfortable position. For, no matter how much one refuses to identify with the caricature that is offered by Nietzsche when he says some of his more outrageous things about Jews or women, these caricatures teach us something important about what it means to not be of the majority—namely, that one's identity is not always freely adopted but is sometimes imposed.[24] That the minoritarian Other is not fully empowered to resist the interpellating power that the majority exercises at its whim was a lesson that the "assimilated" and "unreligious" Jews of Europe learned tragically during the reign of Nazism, and it is a lesson that all "minorities" need to recognize if they wish to avoid similar tragedies.

This brings me to my final point, offering a hypothesis concerning why so many Jewish scholars nevertheless are attracted to Nietzsche. This hypothesis appeals to what is perhaps one of the most Semitic of values—namely, that the enemy of my enemy is my friend. Nietzsche's enemy is clearly the hegemonic value system of modernity, a value system that he identifies most closely with Christianity. Insofar as Jews as a persecuted minority have been suffering at the hands of Christians for much of the past two thousand years, perhaps there is more than a little vicarious pleasure to be derived by a Jewish scholar from citing Nietzsche's vitriol directed against the ethico-theological hegemony of Christianity. But it is not *just* vicarious pleasure, I would hasten to add; nor is it mere *ressentiment*, for at least in the United States these days, where we have, perhaps for the first time in our history, a Christian president who in his official duties and pronouncements sees no problem invoking his god as the only god, and when the likes of the Reverends Falwell and Robertson can all but legitimate the terrorist attack on New York City as punishment for its citizens' lack of Christian virtue, more than a few people are seeing in the increasing political hegemony of the Christian-fundamentalist right the signs of an attack against all who think differently.[25] Insofar as what is being attacked are many of the values and programs long taken for granted by both social welfare state leftists and social democratic centrists, it may not only be the Jews who will find critical resources in Nietzsche's declaration of war against a fundamentalist, *ressentiment*-inspired Christianity.

Before I conclude, I would like to make two final comments concerning Sarah Kofman. Kofman became, in her later books, like Nietzsche, a very personal writer. Her last two works—*Le mépris des Juifs* and *Rue Ordener, rue Labat*—show how one might return to the personal as one confronts the question of whether, at this moment in history, it is yet possible for a Jew, or for a woman, to escape an identity that others will not let them escape. Let me then close with two speculative, biographical, and intentionally provocative comments. In discussions of Kofman, it is not uncommon to find her and her work described in terms of being at the intersection of three thinkers: Nietzsche, Freud, and Derrida. I think this is a mistake, and I would like to draw attention to what some of you may have noticed as an absence in my remarks and suggest explicitly that Kofman had only two masters: Nietzsche and Freud. I say she had only two masters because Kofman could have as a master only one who could no longer speak for himself and, insofar as Nietzsche and Freud were both no longer around to contradict what Kofman had them say, she was free to accept them as her masters while using her interpretive genius to make their texts say just what she wanted them to say, or, better, what she herself wanted to say. In this sense, I think it is right to see Kofman's genius at work when she brings *her* Freud to bear on her reading of Nietzsche, and *her* Nietzsche to bear on her reading of Freud. Kofman's relation to Derrida, it seems to me, is quite different, for Derrida, with whom Kofman worked closely for several years, required a certain fidelity, a certain deference, indeed a certain discipleship from those who wished to remain close to him. Perhaps the primary marker of this requirement was the imperative to think with and about Heidegger, and it is not coincidental that those French thinkers most closely aligned with Derrida are also deeply Heideggerian. Sarah Kofman refused this imperative: she refused Heidegger, and she thereby refused to remain within the Derridean fold. She suffered for that refusal, both professionally and, especially, personally.

My second comment may be even more controversial, as it concerns the question of the Jewishness of these four respective thinkers. Kofman is, as I have suggested here, a deeply Jewish thinker. Freud, while a non-believing

Jew, remains on Kofman's reading a Jewish thinker. Nietzsche, a non-believing non-Jew, on Kofman's reading has to become a Jew to become who he is. What, then, of Derrida? Certainly a more religious thinker than either Freud or Nietzsche. But is his religiousness truly Jewish in a way that Kofman would find familiar? And here I think the answer is no, an answer that might seem strange to an American audience. But within the dynamics of French, or perhaps more narrowly, Parisian Jewry, there are significant differences, both cultural and religious, between the Ashkenazi and Sephardic Jews, the Jews of Eastern Europe and the Jews of North Africa. These differences have not been sufficiently attended to in discussions of the relationship between Levinas and Derrida, and they distinguish Kofman's relationship to Jewish traditions and history and Derrida's relations to different Jewish traditions and a different Jewish history. I think these differences put Kofman again closer to Freud, and even to Nietzsche on her construction of him in *Le mépris des Juifs*, than to Derrida, and they may also contribute to our understanding of why Derrida's work has been so well received, where it has been well received, within the American Continental philosophical community, while the Jewishness of thinkers like Levinas and Kofman often passes without comment.

Let me conclude, then, by citing the opening chapter of *Rue Ordener, rue Labat*, translated so beautifully by Ann Smock, which I read as applying not only to this text but to *Le mépris des Juifs* as well:

> Of him all I have left is the fountain pen. I took it one day from my mother's purse, where she kept it along with some other souvenirs of my father. It is a kind of pen no longer made, the kind you have to fill with ink. I used it all through school. It "failed" me before I could bring myself to give it up. I still have it, patched up with Scotch tape; it is right in front of me on my desk and makes me write, write.
>
> Maybe all my books have been the detours required to bring me to write about "that." (Kofman 1996, 3)

Notes

An earlier version of parts of this paper appears in Schrift 1999.

1. See Kofman 1996. When we met, I was not familiar with Kofman's *Paroles suffoquées* (1987). Had I been, I would have recalled immediately its first dedication: *A la mémoire de mon père, mort à Auschwitz.*

2. It warrants recalling as well that two of this century's most important critical analysts of anti-Semitism, the Frankfurt school founders Theodor Adorno and Max Horkheimer, also offer significant reflections on Nietzsche's works that similarly overlook "the Jewish question" in Nietzsche.

3. See *Thus Spoke Zarathustra*, "On Little Old and Young Women," in Nietzsche 1982.

4. See *On the Genealogy of Morals*, essay 1, sec. 16, in Nietzsche 1967; *Beyond Good and Evil*, sec. 195, in Nietzsche 1966; and *Human All Too Human*, sec. 475, in Nietzsche 1986.

5. Kofman 1994b, 49. While I have made use of Duncan Large's unpublished English translation of this text, the responsibility for all translations that appear in what follows is mine.

6. Arendt herself notes that while Nietzsche correctly estimated "the significant role of the Jews in European history," his affirmation of the "'good European' . . . saved him from falling into the pitfalls of cheap philosemitism or patronizing 'progressive' attitudes" (1951, 23).

7. A similar point could be made about Marx, whose early anti-Jewish writings, while they should not be confused with the anti-Semitic writings of some of his contemporaries, may bear some responsibility for the twentieth-century anti-Semitism of some supposed "Marxists."

8. Nietzsche's cultural and political reception in Germany is discussed in a number of recent works, including Aschheim 1992 and Taylor 1990. An earlier and more narrowly focused discussion of Nietzsche's reception by the German left is to be found in Thomas 1983.

9. For a discussion of Kofman's *Nietzsche et la métaphore*, see Schrift 1990, 85–94, 166–68.

10. Cf. *Ecce Homo*, "Why I Write Such Good Books," in Nietzsche 1992.

11. See *On the Genealogy of Morals*, preface, sec. 8, in Nietzsche 1967; *Thus Spoke Zarathustra*, "The Return Home," in Nietzsche 1982; and *Ecce Homo*, "Thus Spoke Zarathustra," sec. 3, in Nietzsche 1992.

12. This and several of the following paragraphs are taken, with minor alterations, from the concluding pages of my *Nietzsche's French Legacy: A Genealogy of Poststructuralism* (New York: Routledge, 1995).

13. *Human, All Too Human*, sec. 475, in Nietzsche 1986.

14. I pursue this point in Schrift 2000 and Schrift 2002.

15. See *On the Genealogy of Morals*, essay 3, sec. 12, in Nietzsche 1967.

16. See also Duffy and Mittelman 1988.

17. See, for example, *Beyond Good and Evil*, sec. 52, in Nietzsche 1966. See also *Human, All Too Human*, sec. 475, in Nietzsche 1986.

18. *On the Genealogy of Morals*, essay 1, sec. 16, in Nietzsche 1967.

19. See Binion 1968, 135–40.

20. Letter to Marie von Schleinitz, May 1878, quoted in Hayman 1980, 204.

21. See Friedrich Nietzsche, *Briefwechsel: Kritische Gesamtausgabe*, ed. Giorgio Colli and Mazzino Montinari, Abt. 3, Bd. 1 (Berlin: Walter de Gruyter, 1981), letters 434, 435.

22. The most notorious example here is, of course, the original version of section 3 of the first chapter of *Ecce Homo*, which Elisabeth prevented from appearing in

the edition of 1905, published five years after Nietzsche's death, in which Nietzsche writes, "I recognize that the deepest objection against the 'eternal recurrence,' my own *most abysmal* thought, are always mother and sister" (Nietzsche 1980, 268).

23. Sarah Kofman cites several of these remarks in the closing chapter of Kofman 1994b, 78–83.

24. Jean-Paul Sartre's *Anti-Semite and Jew* (1970) remains one of the great analyses of this phenomenon.

25. On the September 13, 2001, broadcast of Pat Robertson's Christian television program *The 700 Club*, two days after the attack of September 11, Falwell made the following statement: "I really believe that the pagans, and the abortionists, and the feminists, and the gays and the lesbians who are actively trying to make that an alternative lifestyle, the ACLU, People For the American Way, all of them who have tried to secularize America. I point the finger in their face and say 'you helped this happen'" (qtd. by John F. Harris, "God Gave U.S. 'What We Deserve,' Falwell Says," *Washington Post*, September 14, 2001).

CHAPTER 6

Playing with Fire: Kofman and Freud on Being Feminine, Jewish, and Homosexual

TINA CHANTER

> If the enigma of the text is linked to a disruption, an originary repression, a castration, and the prohibition against contact, one can say that it refers to the enigma par excellence: femininity.
>
> —Kofman, "Le ressemblance des portraits"

One can trace, throughout Sarah Kofman's body of work, a thread of continuity, a question about the unsayable, an enigma, a caesura, a riddle, a disruption, an aporia, the impossibility of saying that which nonetheless, according to an ethical exigency, demands to be said. If in one sense this question can be followed, it also subsides, retreats, withdraws, goes into hiding, disappearing, barricading itself behind various veils, or screens—so many smoke screens, we might say. Much of Kofman's work exhibits an extravagant degree of control. It is the work of a responsible, tenacious scholar, work that proceeds through a meticulous mastery of detail, a schematic presentation that privileges order. The tension between myth and science, death and eros, feminine and masculine, constitutes a ceaseless exchange, but one which does not take place without leaving behind a residue, a remainder. A smoke signal.

I.

Perhaps Kofman is right to criticize Luce Irigaray's reading of Freud in the name of preserving its heterogeneity and complexity. Even the most sympathetic reader of Irigaray's account in *Speculum* must admit that it can be read as tending toward a certain thematic reductiveness. Yet it must also be admitted that this reductiveness is tied to the systems of thought Irigaray mimics, and in mimicking, also distances herself from. The rewards of what might appear to be Irigaray's dogmatically tendentious and monological interpretations include an exposé of Freud's unremitting, yet unacknowledged, unthematized—repressed?—allegiance to an economy governed by masculine homosexuality. Not only does Freud preclude the possibility of a viable female subject, but his foreclosure of this possibility is governed, I would argue, by his own intense anxiety about his "femininity" or, as Kofman has shown, his Jewishness. Noting the link between misogyny and anti-Semitism—"Circumcision is unconsciously equated with castration" (Kofman 1985a, 31 n. 13)—Kofman develops the theme of shame, that supposedly "fundamental" feminine virtue (39). Kofman points to the "shame" Freud feels about the publication of a text, *The Interpretation of Dreams*, which he regards as so "private" that he has "put off" publishing it (Kofman 1985a, 24). She suggests that Freud's delay in publishing *Dreams* is implicated not only in the death of his father; it is not only "taking the father's place 'heroically'" that is at stake, not only the symbolic killing of the father (the identification with Oedipus is made explicit [23]), but this delay is also implicated in his desire for the mother (27). Freud's incestuous desire for the mother is expressed in a dream (29). He is "another Oedipus" although it is only in dreams that he "killed" his father and "slept with his mother" (29). The identification with Oedipus goes as far as echoing both the heroic and the monstrous exhibited in that singular figure. Oedipus is a pharmakos and Freud risks inspiring "horror"—the same response that is provoked by women's genitals, according to Freud. He exposes "along with his own criminal incestuous relations—woman's sex, the mother's sex" (Kofman 1985a, 30). In order that the text not "arouse horror, the reader would have to be familiar with the representation of incest and to have overcome castration anxiety. Freud's willingness to publish this book implies that he himself has overcome such anxiety and by the same token is no longer afraid to expose his *own femininity* as well, that most secret part of his most private being" (30). Freud believes himself to have overcome his fear of femininity—although, as Kofman sees, it is by no means certain that he has done so. Even if he passes himself off as having done so, he will never overcome his fear of homosexuality, whether in his own case, or in the case of his female patients (and Kofman, perhaps, does not see this so clearly). For there can be no female homosexuality without female subjectivity.[1]

So, Freud is working through his relation to his father's death at the same time as he confronts his incestuous desire for his mother. Death and female sexuality have in common the fact that neither of them "can be faced directly" (Kofman 1985a, 20). Freud's anxiety over death "is not 'pure'"—it is contaminated with a fear of sexual impotence, and since woman represents the threat of castration, this means that the question of death is contaminated with the question of woman. Freud's anxiety about death leads him to publish *The Interpretation of Dreams* (22), despite the fact that he has "put off" doing so (24). He wants to achieve "immortality" (23, 25) and to thereby regain youth (23), but he defers gratification of this desire (26). He thereby kills "two birds with one stone: he shows his own superiority to his father, and he punishes himself for succeeding where his father failed" (26).[2]

One crucial result of Freud's cathected relationship to his own femininity is his almost total inability to envisage in any meaningful way the existence of female homosexuality.[3] The effects of this incapacity of Freud do not fail to reemerge, I submit, in the apparent failure of Kofman's own critical powers of reflection—so persuasive elsewhere—when it comes to directly confronting the precise contours of Freud's homophobia. Or, perhaps Kofman's refusal to elaborate thematically that which nevertheless finds its way into her texts should be read less as a failure than as an impetus for the different way of writing that emerges in her autobiographical texts. If there is a certain withdrawal on Kofman's part, at least thematically, from the homosexuality that she writes enigmatically into her autobiographical texts, she also leaves a trace of this withdrawal implicit in her own youthful attachment to the maternal figure, who played such a major, albeit conflictual, role in her own life. If Kofman's scholarly treatment of Freud fails to be sufficiently sensitive to his homophobia, does her later writing succeed in rendering homosexuality enigmatic in a way that comes out against that homophobia? How does this enigma emerge as a conundrum in Kofman's writing of her own life? I develop this question in section 2, below.

About Freud, Kofman says: "The choice of a homosexual object which often characterizes this type of woman is conceived of not as a woman's desire for another woman but actually as a man's desire for another man (for a woman whom she takes in her own image as someone who has a penis, since she herself identifies with her phallic mother or father [*sic*]" (1985a 204). At this point in the text, in a footnote, Kofman makes her only purely positive assessment of Irigaray's reading of Freud in *Enigma,* saying simply, "In this regard Luce Irigaray speaks very aptly of 'hommosexualité'" (204 n. 32). This is indeed one of Irigaray's central and devastating points about Freud. Yet if Kofman concedes it, she does not follow through fully its ramifications—at least not thematically. If there is a sticking point when it comes to Kofman's own homosexuality, it is wrapped up in an enigma, a puzzle, a riddle. I propose that Kofman writes that enigma into her penultimate book, and leaves it there for those who will to read it. Every text is a compromise, says Kofman (see 1988b, 55). Every writer defends himself or herself behind a "bundle of themes" (1991, 162). It is in its very veiling that the text displays what it is hiding. One of the veils in Kofman's works, the screen or mask that displays what it is hiding, is her thematic evasion of homosexuality. It is with this evasion, this unanswered question embedded in Kofman's texts, and left there, smoldering, leaving only smoke trails behind, that this chapter is concerned.

Kofman says of Freud: "Masculine bisexuality is undeniable at the level of object choice, for if man generally retains a single libidinal object . . . he may make a homosexual object choice. Now homosexuality implies bisexuality as the condition that makes it possible" (1985a, 127). Kofman goes on to comment, "It is society, not Freud, that decides here what is 'normal' and what is not; Freud only notes an equal attachment, in the beginning, to masculine or feminine objects, such that heterosexuality, instead of going 'without saying,' being natural and normal, is as problematic as homosexuality" (127). Kofman clearly intends here to be suggesting Freud's liberal attitude toward homosexuality, since her point is to show how heterosexuality is as "problematic" as homosexuality. But insofar as she puts society and Freud on opposite sides of an apparently irreconcilable imaginary divide, she acts as if Freud, and the views he develops, have nothing to do with society. If Freud is simply reacting to social dictum, isn't there also a sense in which his theories help to construct it? Even if we were to agree that he merely confirms what society already postulates, that very confirmation comes to bear a huge responsibility, given the authority that accumulates behind the Freudian legacy. Even if Freud acknowledges that "the exclusive sexual interest felt by men for women is also a problem that needs elucidating and is not a self-evident fact based upon an attraction that is ultimately of a chemical nature" (Kofman 1985a, 127), he still speaks of the need for a "cure" (128).[4] And even if we agree with him that "the cure is the reestablishment of complete bisexual functioning" (Kofman 1985a, 128), so that "a 'pure' heterosexual is as 'sick' as a homosexual," we must also admit that the sense in which this can be true remains theoretical, and that "for social reasons, it rarely turns out that patients on the couch ask to cured of their heterosexuality" (128).

This returns us to the problematic distinction between "Freud," on the one hand, and "society," on the other. For it turns out, of course, that it is only homosexuals who are treated with a view to "restoring" the "full bisexual functions" (128).[5] And even if Freud stipulates that "it lay with him to choose whether he wished to abandon the path that is banned by society," he goes right on to talk of how successful one can be in conversion: "In general to undertake to convert a fully developed homosexual into a heterosexual does not offer much more prospect of success than the reverse, except that for good practical reasons the latter is never attempted" (Kofman 1995a, 128). The "good practical reasons" are none other than those offered by society, whether in the form of a simple social convention, or in the form of a concern, often expressed by Freud, about the continuation and preservation of the species.[6] In either case, the alleged divide between Freud and society, between psychoanalysis and "good practical reasons," suffers severe compromise, if it does not break down entirely. When Kofman comments, "Psychoanalysis learns not only that heterosexuality could not be the psychic norm (although it is indeed the social norm) but that there is no such thing as pure heterosexuality" (1985a, 128), one wonders about the legitimacy of speaking as if "psychic" and "social" norms can be unproblematically said to maintain their integrity.

Kofman is attentive to Freud's Jewishness and his humble origins—which provide an echo of her own working-class identifications—(Freud often referred to himself as a "poor Jew"). Kofman is also sensitive to a certain complicity that pertains between his troubled relationship to femininity and his ongoing attempt to negotiate the fact of his Jewishness.[7] This complicity, I suggest, can be articulated by an interrogation of Freud's conception of homosexuality, a notion that, in its turn—at least at the thematic level—seems not to trouble Kofman enough. There is, in Freud, an insistent, yet neglected, reference running through his work on the feminine, a motif that accompanies the discourse that accumulates around the concept of homosexuality. That motif concerns the antithesis Freud sets up between fire and water (see Freud 1932, 190), playing with that all-important ancient discovery of fire by putting it out in time-honored means—through micturation, with all the phallic overtones that comply with this act of playful mastery. In section 3, by following through this motif, which crops up in some of the most decisive texts in Freud's corpus (on Dora [see 1905a], on the wolf man [see 1918a], and in "Civilization and Its Discontents" [1930]), I hope, in passing, to shed some new light—or at least disperse some old smoke—on some issues that have preoccupied feminist engagements with psychoanalysis.[8]

II.

> *[W]riting* [is] supremely unheimlich because it repeats in symbolic form the forbidden sexual act: "As soon as writing, which entails making a liquid flow out of a tube onto a piece of white paper, assumes the significance of copulation, or as soon as walking becomes a symbolic substitution for treading upon the body of mother earth, both writing and walking are stopped, because they represent the performance of a forbidden sexual act" . . . writing is a diabolical production.
>
> —Kofman, *Freud and Fiction*

"Our reunion was idyllic . . . we slept in the same bed, in her room, in order not to be separated . . . I remember especially the first night, when my emotion and excitement were very great. Just to feel so close to her put me into an 'odd' state. I was hot, I was thirsty, I was blushing. I kept mum, and really I would have been hard put to say anything about it, since I had no idea what was happening to me" (Kofman 1996, 67).[9]

Kofman records in this passage her reunion with the woman she called Mémé, who hid her and her mother from the Nazis during World War Two. The account occurs in the autobiographical work, one of the last books she was to write, *Rue Ordener, rue Labat*. Mémé, a neighbor and a non-Jew, became a second mother to Kofman, and in fact she even won a legal battle to gain parental rights to Kofman. This was not an unusual occurrence in war-weary Europe, as Miep Gies, one of Anne Frank's helpers, testifies.[10] Against the law, Kofman's mother refuses to give Sarah up. Despite the profound affection Kofman felt for Mémé—from whom she did not want to be separated—Kofman registers the relief she felt at her mother's refusal to capitulate to the law. "I struggled, cried, sobbed. Deep down, I was relieved" (Kofman 1996, 61). Earlier in the same text Kofman writes about the anxiety she experienced in being separated from her birth mother, an anxiety manifested in repeated vomiting (see 1996, 30). Kofman begins the section titled "Separations" thus: "The real danger: separation from my mother" (27), and goes on to recount a time "between the ages of two and three years old" at which she "lost sight of" her mother "for a few moments" (27). Kofman's vomiting is closely imbricated in her refusal to give up give up her allegiance to Jewish taboos on eating certain foods, especially pork, and her consequent jeopardizing not only of her own safety, but also that of her sister, Rachel, who was passing for Christian (sec 1996, 24). In order that her Jewish identity not be found out, Kofman had to dissimulate, to eat pork (see 1996, 21, 31). Her inability to keep down the prohibited food is, in turn, bound up with the law of her father, a rabbi, whose death at Auschwitz Kofman briefly recounts as the beginning of *Rue Ordener, rue Labat*. Kofman perverts the Judaic law, the law of the father, for her own ends, constituting it as a refusal to be separated from her mother.[11] Kofman's anxieties about being separated from her mother were so acute that while her brothers and sisters stayed in the country, where it was safer, Kofman had to be returned to her mother. Kofman moves back to Paris, where she begins to "pass" as Mémé's daughter (Kofman 1996, 40).

In contrast to Kofman's memory of the night in which she stayed in the same bed as Mémé—a night of which she has, however, no knowledge: "I had no idea what was happening to me"—she has no memory of an earlier occasion when she "slept in the same bed" as Mémé. All she remembers is that "Mémé got undressed behind a big mahogany screen" and that she, Kofman, was "fascinated by her bare breasts" (1996, 55). Kofman draws attention to this fascination and this failure of memory by using the subheading "screen" for her recounting of the episode. A screen-memory then? "Knowingly or not," says Kofman, accounting for the intensity of her relationship to Mémé, "Mémé had brought off a tour de force: right under my mother's nose, she'd managed to detach me from her. And also from Judaism" (47). Her father gone, Mémé performed for Kofman the role that would normally have fallen to the father, reenacting the first separation from the mother, a function ascribed by Freud and Lacan to the paternal metaphor. That Kofman expresses the blatant "tour de force"—or is it rather a coup d'état?—in terms of its being "right under my mother's nose" is significant, given that Mémé reminded Kofman of her Jewish nose, a fact that Kofman records in the context of her remark that Mémé was not without anti-Semitism (see 1996, 47). In *Smothered Words*, Kofman writes about Maurice Blanchot's short story that in "The Idyll" "everything is always ambiguous. There is a time for work, but *also* [*aussi*] a time for celebration: an 'also' [aussi]—the very mark of time, of continuity—is always possible" (1998b 33; 1987c, 41).

The later of the two scenes to which I have alluded, in which Kofman expresses her desire not to be separated from Mémé, the one in which her memory serves her but her knowledge fails, was, Kofman relates, an "idyllic" reunion. The section of *Rue Ordener, rue Labat* in which she describes it is titled simply "Idyll." In *Smothered Words* Kofman gives a reading of Blanchot's "The Idyll" in which she explores the "law" (1998b, 15; 1987c, 22) or "economy" (1998b, 17; 1987c, 24) of the story, its "idyllic law" (1998b, 17; 1987c, 24), "the omnipotence of the law . . . and of its idyllic memory" (1998b, 21; 1987c, 28). "'The Idyll' is a title that permits every form of continuity" says Kofman (1998b, 31; 1987c, 39). Elsewhere Kofman points to the connection between eros and continuity (see 1988b, 55).

The key question that Kofman asks in *Smothered Words* is, "How can testimony escape the idyllic law of the story?" (1998b, 36; 1987c, 43). She is interested in the "ethical demand that communicates with the exigency of the highest writing, breaking with all idyllic language" (1998b, 31; 1987c, 39). The close proximity between Levinas and this Blanchot-inspired text by Kofman is hardly coincidental, given the deep philosophical continuity—and discontinuity—between Blanchot and Emmanuel Levinas.[12] A "relation without relation" (see Kofman 1998b, 53; 1987c, 61) one might say, but not a community without community (see 1998b, 70; 1987c, 79).[13] Kofman dedicates *Smothered Words* to the memory of her father, to Blanchot, and to Robert Antelme. Antelme's book *The Human Race* (*L'espèce humaine*) is an account of his survival of Dachau. Blanchot calls it sublime. Inspired by Blanchot, Kofman writes, hesitating to use the word "humanism" (but using it all the same), that it is a "trite and idyllic" word. She thus uses the word as she effaces it, in a gesture that is reminiscent of the crossing out of Being; she uses it to rewrite humanism, as Levinas uses the word "metaphysics," writing out its history in order to introduce a new history, a new meaning for the word. She uses it in the sense that Blanchot, as Kofman's reading of "The Idyll" reveals (without revealing—see Kofman 1998b, 27; 1987c, 33), writes a story that implies what he will explicitly articulate in the 1973 text *The Madness of the Day*, namely, that there are no more stories (see Kofman 1998b, 14–15; 1987c, 14–15).[14]

Just so, Kofman writes of a humanism that is longer a humanism. I do not think that her use of the term "humanism," or her announcement of a "new ethics" (1998b, 73; 1987c, 82), amounts to a capitulation of her earlier admonishment, following (according to Dobie) Adorno (but not only Adorno—also Blanchot and Levinas), not to endorse a totalizing "dialectization" (Kofman 1998b, xix),[15] any more than Blanchot's stories cannot be said to be real stories, because they interrupt the law of the idyll. They are stories, and they are no longer stories, in that, precisely as stories, they challenge what have come to be known as stories, that with which we are comfortable and familiar, that with which we find ourselves at home. They are *unheimlich*.[16] Their strangeness is such that they remind us of the familiar, and in doing so they also call attention to the dissonance of their being no longer what they were. "Continuity bespeaks discontinuity. . . . It is in its very veiling that the text displays what it is hiding" (Kofman 1988b, 55).

Let us return to the two mothers of Kofman, a return that will involve a brief detour involving two other mothers, those of Leonardo da Vinci. "The artist," writes Kofman in *Rue Ordener*, "seems to have used the blissful smile of St. Anne to disavow and to cloak the envy which the unfortunate woman felt when she was forced to give up her son to her better-born rival, as she had once given up his father" (1996, 64).[17] Kofman sandwiches this passage—a passage that all but reproduces one in *The Childhood of Art* (see 1988b, 82)—and where, significantly, she goes on to discuss Leonardo's relationship to "a forbidden, homosexual love" (1988b, 84)—between the two passages with which I began this section, between her memory and her failed memory, her screened, cloaked, veiled, unconscious, masked memory, a memory that in its veiling displays what it is hiding. These two memories play out the conflict between the good and the bad mother, the good and the bad breast.[18] A continuity is thus established between Kofman's two mothers, her more protracted discussion of Leonardo's two mothers, and Freud's uncanny, double relation to his mother. Kofman's own experience (or her nonexperience—her trauma) as a child, consisted of her incapacity to pay any regard to her mother's pain and jealousy. Like Leonardo's mother, Kofman's mother also felt forced to give up her child (in this case a daughter) "to a better-born rival, as she had once been forced to give up her father" (to whom, to the god who died at Auschwitz?). Mémé was better born in the sense of chance, fate, or luck—the luck of being born, in the era of the Holocaust, Christian, rather than Jewish; Kofman's mother had lost her husband at Auschwitz. Kofman had been deprived of the normative function even this feminized father would have played in effecting her separation, however complex and incomplete it would have been, from her mother, who is forced to cede that dubious task to her rival—and her savior—Mémé. Mémé, the substitute mother, in a curious way, and completely unintentionally, through an accident of birth, has unmanned and dethroned Kofman's Jewish father.

Rue Ordener, rue Labat opens with a passage entitled "The Fountain Pen." Kofman says of her father, "All I have left is the fountain pen . . . I still have it, patched up with Scotch tape; it is right in front of me on my desk and makes me, write, write" (1996, 3). Kofman describes a postcard that her father had sent to the family, written in the hand of another, and in French, from Auschwitz, in which he "asked that in the two-kilogram packages we were legally authorized to send we be sure to include cigarettes. And he asked my mother," Kofman continues, "to take good care of the baby" (9). The card was the last one they were to receive from him. It was the "last sign of life" (9), says Kofman. And she adds that after her mother's death it proved impossible to locate the card, which Kofman "had reread so often," and that "she wanted to save." It was, she says, "as if I had lost my father a second time, from then on nothing was left" (9). Somehow, between the first page of the text and the recounting of the disappearance of this last sign of life from Kofman's father, something else has been lost. A supplementary loss. The fountain pen, which Kofman says is still on her desk, which makes her write, is gone. Forgotten. Shades of Derrida's *Spurs*, and the forgotten umbrella, the stylus? "From then on nothing was left," says Kofman, discounting the pen.

The translator Madeleine Dobie comments on the fact that some of the quotes have been misattributed, that Kofman may have been distracted, due to the subject matter, and duly corrects the footnotes wherever possible (see 1998b, xxiv–xxv). Can the same be said of this "mistake" in *Rue Ordener, rue Labat*? Perhaps; but I prefer to see Kofman's unconscious at work here. What has happened when Kofman writes, "From then on nothing was left"? What has happened to the pen? Is this a simple slip of the tongue, of the pen? Surely not, since the fountain pen (which, not incidentally, she stole from her mother's purse) was so important to Kofman that she kept it, albeit "patched up," on her desk all the time she was writing.[19] And she was writing all the time: "[I]t makes me write, write." Although it did not work, the pen made her write. Perhaps because it had fallen into disuse, it made her write. Due to her father's death, she must write. Perhaps she was compensating, with her writing, for her father's death? Displacing her mourning? The card, which turned out to be the writing on the wall, writing her father was not allowed to write for himself, writing penned in the hand of another, is gone. The pen, deprived of its function, merely present-at-hand, is no longer used. Kofman's father is no longer here to use it. So Kofman must write in his stead. And as she writes, her writing, eventually, becomes a mourning. After which, perhaps, she could let go.

Kofman comments, briefly and indirectly, at the end of "The Fountain Pen" that her writing has changed. She suggests that perhaps all her writing was for this—this autobiographical work that she begins to write with an account of her father's death. As if all the other careful, painstaking, scholarly writing, on Freud, Nietzsche, Comte, and so many others, had come to this. As if it were all merely a passageway to this. Something she had to get out of her system. Or, a system she had to get out of her writing? For, as Ann Smock observes, this is a different kind of writing.[20] It is not a writing of mastery. It flows freely, it is more disjointed, more poetic. More unconscious? Idyllic, we might say. It seems to escape Kofman in some ways. It is uncontrollable. In Smock's words, this writing is "bathed in a lucidity unclouded by insight" (Kofman 1996, xii). Usually the consummate scholar, something breaks in Kofman. A breakthrough. A breaking through of the death of her father? A breaking through of a death to come?

Kofman writes in *Rue Ordener, rue Labat* that "cigarettes were the one thing [her father] couldn't do without."[21] She recalls how, when cigarettes were hard to come by during the war years, she "used to pick up cigarette butts for him on the sidewalk, and liked to go to the Rue Jean-Robert to buy him the zig-zag papers he used to roll his cigarettes." She adds, in a new and final paragraph to "Zig-Zag" (the title of this short section), that "Later, in a dream" her father "appeared . . . as a drunk zigzagging across the street" (1996, 12). She does not say how much later, but if it was during the inner struggle, later developing into an outer struggle, and finally becoming a legal battle, between her mother and Mémé, perhaps the dream can be interpreted in terms of Kofman's metaphorically being pulled from the rue Orderner to the rue Labat, zigzagging from one street to another, emotionally divided between one mother and the other, between two mothers. Like Leonardo. Symbolically, being drunk for Freud, as Kofman notes in *Enigma* (1985a, 26) means making love.[22] So, was Kofman's father symbolically making love to her "two" mothers?

Kofman says of her father, "At home, as soon as the Sabbath was over, he would light one up. The rule against smoking on that day was especially hard on him" (1996, 11). Darkness would "put an end to his ordeal. Then he would light a twisted red candle, saying the kiddush with a glass of wine in his hand; then he extinguished the candle with the overturned glass and lit the electric lights. Then he would smoke" (11).

The trail of smoke left behind by Kofman's father leads us back to another smoker. To Freud. And to Dora—and thus to Dora's father and to Herr K., both of whom Freud identifies with, as he tells us in the case history of Dora when he relates his interpretation of Dora's first dream, in which Dora dreams that "*A house was on fire*" (1905a, 64). Freud says, that in an "addendum to the dream," which she had at first "forgotten to relate," Dora tells him that each time after this recurrent dream "after waking up she had smelt smoke" (65). Freud goes on: "Smoke, of course, fitted in well with fire, but it also showed that the dream had a special relation to myself; for when she used to assert that there was nothing concealed behind this or that, I would often say by way of rejoinder: 'There is no smoke without fire!' Dora objected, however, to such a purely personal interpretation, saying that Herr K. and her father were passionate smokers—as I am too, for the matter of that. She herself had smoked during her stay by the lake, and Herr K. had rolled a cigarette for her before he began his unlucky proposal" (73). After adding a few more details, Freud suggests that "the addendum to the dream could scarcely mean anything else than the longing for a kiss, which, with a smoker would necessarily smell of smoke. . . . Taking into consideration, finally, the indications which seemed to point to there having been a transference on to me—since I am a smoker too—I came to the conclusion that the idea had probably occurred to her one day during a sitting that she would like to have a kiss from me" (73–74). One can see why feminist interpretations have had trouble with Freud's failure to deal very successfully with the issue of transference in the case of Dora!

But I want to go elsewhere, at least for the moment. In an essay that she calls "It's only the first step that costs," Kofman relates Freud's passion (and surely Freud was a father figure for Kofman, who wrote so many books on his work) for speculation, his smoking, and the fact of his Jewishness, taking note of the connection between smoking, writing, and his Jewishness (see Kofman 1994a). She recalls the dream Freud writes that he had in *The Interpretation of Dreams*, following his father's death, in which he sees written on a poster "You are requested to close the eyes" or "You are requested to close an eye," which "reminds him of the 'Smoking is prohibited' notices that are found in station waiting rooms" (Kofman 1994a, 110). Kofman goes on, "Nor is it coincidental that at the moment when he can no longer smoke as he pleases—the moment it would have cost him dearly to do so—he says that he no longer has any desire to write" (110). The price, the cost, the loss of writing is a theme that often emerges in Kofman's work on Freud. And the motif of smoke is never far away. Where there is writing, there are smoke screens.

No smoke appears in *Smothered Words*, only the "writing of ashes" (1998b, 8; 1987c, 14), "ashes from Auschwitz," "children reduced to ashes who were not permitted to speak, to have a story, and who were not, at their death returned to their mothers," "All the ashes upon the soil of Auschwitz," "Silence of ashes spread across a plain (1998b, 40; 1987c, 47).[23] If in *Smothered Words*, there are only ashes, that might be because the words have already been choked back, smoked out. There is plenty of smoke to be discerned throughout Freud's writings, and although Kofman does not focus on it in *Enigma*, she does mention its counterpart: water, urine, micturation (see 1985a, 23). Freud pays considered attention to the "antithesis of 'water' and 'fire' (Freud 1905a, 72) in his case history of Dora, which he judges to have been "extremely useful" to Dora in her dream, concluding that she was "addicted to bed-wetting" (72), and returning to the antithesis in later texts. The case history of Dora is, of course, one of Freud's most sustained and celebrated commentaries on a woman, and one of the most controversial in relation to debates over psychoanalysis and homosexuality. Freud's inability to deal with Dora's homosexuality has been much discussed by distinguished feminist critics, such as Hélène Cixous, Suzanne Gearhart, and Jacqueline Rose.[24] Before turning briefly to Kofman's *The Childhood of Art* and Freud's "The Acquisition and Control of Fire," I'd like to turn obliquely and all too briefly to this problematic and rich case history, which has become a centerpiece for any feminist interested in pursuing Freud and Lacan, by following the trail of smoke that Freud leaves in his wake, which, strangely enough, seems to have been left to disappear into thin air. At least in the case of Dora.

Critics have focused on the theme of transference, and made connections between Freud's neglect of, or retreat from, the indications of homosexuality that Dora introduces into her analysis, but which Freud resolutely subordinates to footnotes, added eighteen years after the case history was initially published in 1905.[25] As far as I know, Kofman has not written on the Dora case at any length. But in her essay on Hoffmann's "The Sandman" she makes a point that echoes many a feminist commentator on the case of Dora: Freud once again writes the mother out of the picture.[26] Freud, so conscientious in seeing fire where there was smoke in almost every other matter, so magical at interpreting the symbolic meaning of dreams, so masterful in reading causes from symptoms, took Dora at her word when it came to her mother. He takes Dora's and Dora's father's word for it that Dora's mother, whom Freud never met, was what Freud nonetheless describes as an "uncultivated" and "foolish" woman (1905a, 20).[27] Just as "the importance of the figure of the mother is occluded both by Hoffmann in his story and by Freud in his interpretation"—which, by contrast, in Kofman's words, she has "emphasized" in her essay on Freud's reading of Hoffmann "on several occasions" (Kofman 1991, 161), so Freud wrote the mother out of the picture in his case history of Dora. In Hoffmann's "The Sandman," the diabolical alchemy in which Coppelius is involved—and in which he once involved Nathaniel's father—results in Olympia, a life-size doll, who comes to replace Nathaniel's love for Clara. Nathaniel likes to read his work to Olympia. Unlike Clara, Olympia does not get distracted by other tasks while he reads to her "everything he had ever has written," (Hoffmann 1982, 117), but rather sits there quietly. "What he wants is a frigid, lifeless woman," says Kofman, "a mirror of himself, who will listen to his poems without growing weary" (1991, 143). But, writes Kofman,

> Freud, who is normally so attentive to processes of inversion, remains on the level of the manifest text of the story and, like the story, he emphasizes the figure of the father and his doubles, neglecting even those details which

> could set him on the track of another interpretation (for example, the maternal nature of the sandman, who tears out children's eyes as food for his [own] little children).
>
> If the whole story can be read as a screen-fantasy concealing the incestuous desire for the mother and the threat of death which results from this desire, one might ask whether Hoffmann's insistence on the father's uncanniness, on the theme of paternal double, is not, in fact a diabolical artifice designed to mask a quite different uncanniness, that of *writing* itself, supremely *unheimlich* because it repeats in symbolic form the forbidden sexual act. (1991, 161)[28]

Quoting Hoffmann again, Kofman reproduces the passage, reminiscent of her own description of her father's smoking (see Kofman 1996, 11), in which evening family gatherings are described: "Our father smoked and drank a large glass of beer. Often he told us stories and became so excited over them that his pipe went out and I h[a]d to relight it for him with a burning spill, which I found a great source of amusement. But often he handed us picture books, sat silent and motionless in his armchair and blew out thick clouds of smoke, so that we were all enveloped as if by a fog" (1991, 155).[29]

"There can be no smoke without fire" (Freud 1905a, 73). Freud includes this phrase twice in his writing up of Dora's case history. The first time, as we saw, is in his interpretation of Dora's first dream. He tells this to Dora. Signals require interpretation, we understand. Signs, mythic signals, need to be linked together, concatenated, given meaning, systematized. And the meaning they should be given is Freud's. The second time the phrase occurs, it is to reaffirm Freud's interpretation (despite Dora's protest). In fact, Freud's "proverb, 'There can be no smoke without fire,'" is said to be brought by Dora "very ingeniously into the completed form of the dream" (Freud 1905a, 93). Despite herself, Dora confirms Freud's views. Signs become meaningful. Enigmas are ironed out, closure achieved.[30] But Kofman, as we have seen, is struggling between these two poles, between life and death, between myth and science, which are inseparably linked, and which can only be separated theoretically. For writing is always, as Kofman acknowledges, a compromise, within which the tension sustained between these poles is worked out. Or not.

III.

> There happened to be a large match-stand on the table. I asked Dora to look around and see whether she noticed anything special on the table, something that was not there as a rule. She noticed

> nothing. I then asked her if she knew why children were forbidden to play with matches.
>
> "Yes; on account of the risk of fire. My uncle's children are very fond of playing with matches."
>
> "Not only on that account. They are warned not to 'play with fire,' and a particular belief is associated with the warning."
>
> She knew nothing about it.—"Very well, then; the fear is that if they do they will wet their bed. The antithesis of 'water' and 'fire' must be at the bottom of this. Perhaps it is believed that they will dream of fire and then try and put it out with water."
>
> —Freud, "Fragment of an Analysis of a Case of Hysteria"

In "Civilization and Its Discontents" Freud comments that among "the first acts of civilization . . . the control over fire stands out as a quite extraordinary and unexampled achievement" (1930, 37). Over and above "the use of tools" and "the construction of dwellings" there can be no doubt, says Freud, about the significance of this unparalleled accomplishment. In an extended footnote, Freud elaborates on the phallic character of "tongues of flame as they shoot upwards" and ventures the conjecture that

> primal man had the habit, when he came in contact with fire, of satisfying an infantile desire connected with it, by putting it out with a stream of his urine. . . . Putting out fire by micturating . . . was therefore a kind of sexual act with a male, an enjoyment of sexual potency in a homosexual competition. The first person to renounce this desire and spare the fire was able to carry it off with him and subdue it to his own use. By damping down the fire of his own sexual excitation, he had tamed the natural force of fire. This great cultural conquest was thus the reward for his renunciation of instinct. Further, it is as though woman had been appointed guardian of the fire which was held captive on the domestic hearth, because her anatomy made it impossible for her to yield to the temptation of this desire. (37 n. 1)

I want to underline a number of points about this passage, in which are enshrined several preoccupations of Freud.

The phallic character of the "tongues of flame" that "shoot upwards" is mimicked by the urination by which males compete with one another to extinguish fire. In order to make use of fire, to capitalize on it, this phallic function, the "sexual potency" of a phallic competition among males, a competitive economy that Freud marks as explicitly homosexual, must be renounced; desire must be dampened. Homosexuality must be repressed in order that fire can be retained. Fire comes to substitute for sexual desire—specifically, it stands in for homosexual desire. Henceforth, for civilization to endure (given the enormous weight that Freud attaches to the control of fire) desire must be heterosexual, and homosexuality must be banished to the primeval, uncivilized chaos of prehistory, where men, according to the story that Freud tells, had not yet distinguished their "lives from those of our animal ancestors" (1930, 36). If male homosexuality is dispensed with by means of repression, female homosexuality is rendered unthinkable in another way. Woman is "appointed guardian of the fire which was held captive on the domestic hearth"—not because woman lacks the desire to put out the fire, for she too is tempted, but because "her anatomy made it impossible for her to yield to the temptation of this desire." Woman's desire is the same as man's—homosexual—but her anatomy renders her unable to give in to its temptations. She lacks the means to do so. There is, as all good Freudians know, only one libido, and that libido is masculine. True to form, Freud also adheres to his thesis of bisexuality here. Homosexuality is renounced, repressed, but not entirely abolished. Men overcome homosexual desire, while women, it would seem, cannot even realize it. Thus, by introducing the issue of temptation, and by implication the attendant manifestation of guilt, Freud announces a theme to which he will turn explicitly, and at length, in several key texts—namely, the development of the superego, the differential development of which decisively informs his account of femininity as falling short of masculinity.[31]

Women want what men want—our desire is their desire, our temptation is their temptation, but whereas men overcome temptation, women cannot even yield to it, restricted by anatomy. Women can hardly compete with one another, in a ritual of homosexual competitive bonding, by urinating on fires. Women can hardly develop ethically, in accord with an effective superego, if they cannot do what tempts them anyway. Nor can they therefore sublimate what they cannot even realize at the level of the bodily schema. This, at least, is Freud's contention.

The subtext here is: you need a penis in order to be a homosexual. You need a penis to urinate competitively. And you need a penis in order to be able to represent your instinctual, homosexual, desire, the better to overcome it. Civilized men are those who have transcended the animality of homosexual desire, who have transformed their instinctual desire through sublimating it, allowing the penis to become a signifier, endowing it with a representation of suspended desire, in short, giving the penis the status of the phallus. Civilized men have overcome the instinctual bond with other men for the good of civilization; for the purpose of sustaining cultured life, they have redirected their energies into cultural achievements and scientific discoveries. They have confronted the horror that women inspire in them by threatening castration.[32] They have agreed to enact desire as heterosexual. And for this they are to be congratulated. Not that men's repudiation of instinctual desire is to be seen as an easy, finite, or accomplished task. On the contrary, those libidinal desires will turn out to be not merely persistent, but (adhering to a rule that Freud enunciates in "On Narcissism") indestructible, which only serves to underscore the necessity of their renunciation (see Freud 1932, 191).[33] At the same time, this renunciation, so apparently necessary for "civilized" life, sheds light on the ongoing struggle that characterizes men's attempt to overcome the oedipal complex, a struggle that, to the extent that the superego inherits that conflict, comes to be embodied in the relationship between the ego and superego, and is thus played out in terms of the moral development of the individual.

If fire is a phallic substitute, the dwelling-house is a "substitute for the mother's womb," that "first lodging, for which in all likelihood man still longs, and in which he was safe and felt at ease" (1930, 38).[34] Freud here espouses his belief (to which he returns spasmodically) that the boy's desire for the mother is never fully displaced, thus casting doubt on the successful resolution of the oedipal complex, and at the same time, although perhaps inadvertently, casting doubt upon the decisive differentiation between men and women. If the retarded development of the superego is allegedly symptomatic of women, to open the question of the degree to which the superego develops in men is to reopen the question of sexual difference.[35] Here too, indirectly, the issue of primary narcissism is raised, since what is at stake here is how far the boy has managed to separate from the mother, to what extent he has managed to break up the mother-child dyad, the mythic status of which does not prevent its lasting significance.[36]

The link between controlling fire and renouncing homosexuality that Freud establishes in his footnote to "Civilization and Its Discontents" is no isolated aberration. In 1931, the year after "Civilization and Its Discontents," Freud writes an article called "The Acquisition and Control of Fire" in which he elaborates his thesis. He reiterates his hypothesis that "in order to gain control over fire, men had to renounce the homosexually-tinged desire to put it out with a stream of urine" (1932, 187) and finds confirmation of it in the myth of Prometheus.[37] Not all the details of the myth fit his earlier interpretation, but Freud is not to be deterred by such details. He simply reads the myth as he would a dream, establishing that we must expect a certain amount of "distortion" to occur "in the transition from the facts to the contents of a myth" just like the distortions that occur in dream symbolism. Recalling, then, that Prometheus "brought fire to men, having stolen it from the gods, hidden in a hollow stick, a fennel-stalk," Freud feels justified in interpreting the myth as if it were a dream. He goes on, "If we were interpreting a dream we should be inclined to regard such an object as a penis symbol. . . . But how can we bring this penis-tube into connection with the preservation of fire?" "There seems little chance of doing this," Freud continues, "till we remember the procedure of reversal, of turning into the opposite, of inverting relationships, which is so common in dreams and which so often conceals their meaning from us. What a man harbors in his penis-tube is not fire. On the contrary, it is the means of *quenching* fire; it is the water of his stream of urine" (188).

In appealing to the necessity in dream analysis to turn every element into its opposite, Freud harks back to the much earlier text, "Fragment of an Analysis of a Case of Hysteria" (1905), the very text that has played such a pivotal role in the feminist reception of Freud.[38] Perhaps not coincidentally, Freud's famous analysis of the case of Dora not only contains rich resources as an etiology of hysteria, and as a discourse on transference and countertransference, but it also anticipates Freud's remarkable, yet neglected, essay "The Acquisition of Fire." While the case of Dora has been much scrutinized, the antithesis of fire and water that plays a pivotal role in it seems to have gone unremarked. In the light of the later, explicit connection Freud establishes between homosexuality and fire, I suggest that such a connection can be read back into the analysis of Dora, and that bringing out its relevance not only contributes to the history of feminist readings of Dora, but can also serve as a way of reintroducing the complex and contested relationship between the real, the symbolic, and the imaginary. It also returns us to the firey, "odd," "hot," state that sleeping in the same bed as Mémé put Kofman, the state that made her so "thirsty," making her "blush," the state in which she has "no idea of what was happening" to her.

Freud's lengthy discussion of the superego in "Civilization and Its Discontents" (1930) and "The Ego and the Id" (1923) circle around the question of whether the commission of acts is crucial to guilt administered by the superego. What is the difference, from the point of view of my guilt, between my desire to kill the father, when I do not actually do it, and the killing of the father? Freud says, "[W]hether one has killed one's father or has abstained from doing so is not really the decisive thing. One is bound to feel guilty in either case" (1930, 79) and he asserts that due to the "omniscience of the super-ego, the difference between an aggression intended and an aggression carried out lost its force" (84). Freud points out a "peculiarity" of the conscience, that is, the fact that the more virtuous one is, the more severe is the superego.[39] Freud is particularly interested in the omniscience of the superego, from which, unlike parental authority, one cannot hide. Once authority is internalized as the superego, a "great change takes place," says Freud, since "nothing can be hidden from the superego" (72). But is Freud right about this? Is there really no hiding from the superego? Take homophobia. Take the socially available text of homophobia that is part of the woof and warp of "normal" society. Take the internalization and socialization of psyches. Is it really true that one could not hide, even from oneself, one's true desire? And can we really tell apart the question of whether one knows one's true desire, that central psychoanalytic quest, from the screens and veils and masks we throw up, in our lives, as well as our writing, to shield ourselves from childhood memories, from trauma, from truth, from fiction, in all its uncanniness?

A great deal more could be said about the various contradictions Freud raises concerning the superego, the imaginary and symbolic landscape of femininity in Freud's geography that is shaped by his belief in the inferiority of women's superegos, and the ways in which the superego parallels and differs from parental authority. But I want to underline here the continuity between the question of the reality of the primal scene and the question of "whether one has already done the bad thing or only intends to do it" (Freud 1930, 71).[40] As is well known, at several points in his work Freud famously relates that he has rethought his original position vis-à-vis childhood memories of the primal scene.[41] He now regards such memories as fabrications, as myths, as fictional, whereas previously he had suggested that these memories were based on reality. Furthermore, in his discussion of the Dora case Freud asserts, in accordance with the heterosexual normativity of the oedipal complex, that "the usual sexual attraction had drawn together the father and the daughter" (1905a, 21), and at the same time says, "A string of reproaches against other people leads one to suspect the existence of a string of self-reproaches with the same content" (35). Taking these two assertions together, we find that, despite her "disgust" (25), Dora is understood by Freud to have more or less invited Herr K. to kiss her. And indeed, Freud arrives at a point in the analysis at which, notwithstanding her previous denial, Dora "admitted that she might have been in love with Herr K." (37). Freud thus neatly sidesteps the alleged facts—that Herr K., having engineered things so that he was alone with Dora, "suddenly clasped the girl to him and pressed a kiss upon her lips" (28). Freud interprets this event as a "situation" likely to "call up a distinct feeling of sexual excitement in a girl of fourteen who had never before been approached" (28), instead of seeing that such a girl might feel violated by her father's friend, and, as Dora herself said, disgusted. Such events are written off by Freud as fantasy, as delusional, as stemming, in fact, from Dora's hidden desire to have a kiss from a smoker (Freud, Herr K., Dora's father?). In the series of associations Freud establishes, the direction of Dora's desire is unclear. As long as it is a man, a father figure, it really does not matter that much; as long as it is not Frau K., everything is fine: the heterosexual norm remains firmly in place. Meanwhile, in his discussions of femininity, Freud suggests repeatedly that if anyone was responsible for arousing the child's sexual feelings, it is the mother, in her (rather than the father's) ritual administrations of the child. The responsibility for any violation is therefore placed squarely on the shoulders of mothers.

There is of course a slippage from the potential molestation by a father's friend (a father substitute—insofar as Freud identifies Herr K. with Dora's father) and the inadvertent sexual arousal by the mother as she washes, dresses, or changes the child. But, as we have begun to see, such slippages are in keeping with Freud's tendencies. Freud minimizes the difference between killing the father and thinking of killing the father. Following his logic, why should we not minimize the difference between the father's potential or actual molestation of the child and the mother's inadvertent caresses? After all, it seems clear enough that one of the main reasons for Dora's predicament, actual or real, is certainly her father's affair with Frau K. (Freud 1905a, 32).

For obvious reasons, feminists have taken Freud to task for not believing Dora, and for regarding childhood memories of incest as fantasies. Yet I want to take the risk here of following Freud on this contentious point, at least for a while. Freud's reflections on delusion and fantasy bring us much closer to a feminist imaginary than we might have thought—that, at least, is my contention. What would happen if the imaginary status of childhood beliefs in incestuous events perpetrated by the father figure were to be lined up with Freud's involved discussions of whether or not there is any difference between killing the father and the desire to kill the father? Why does Freud insist upon this ambivalence? Because there is a sense in which it does not matter whether the killing of the father by the primal horde is symbolic or actual. It matters to the father—but not to the primal horde, that band of brothers who must, eventually, atone for their sins by erecting a token, a symbol, a fetish, no less, to make up for their deadly deed. They are guilty whether they carry out the murder, or whether they symbolically kill the father. Freud knows only too well about this, and Kofman follows in detail Freud's ambivalent struggle with his father, whom Freud both surpasses (kills) and atones for, killing two birds with one stone (see Kofman 1985a, 26).

If it matters little whether the killing of the father is symbolic or real, there is also a sense in which it matters little to the child whether or not incest was real or imagined, or whether the primal scene was in fact witnessed, or "only" imagined. Only in a sense, I want to emphasize, for it is painfully obvious that the trauma of real victims of incest is not to be equated with that of imaginary victims; there are, after all serious legal, psychic, and emotional repercussions not only for real victims, but also for anyone accused of molestation. The question of their reality must be, in that sense, decisive. Still, I want to stay with the sense in which the imaginary legitimation of the symbolic realm, whether in the case of a delusion or fantasy, or in the case of an actual event, remains the same.

What if Freud is right, and whether or not Dora is telling the truth is not the most decisive point? What if the decisive point is not what actually happened, but why Dora believes it to have happened, and what is responsible for her delusion, if indeed it is a delusion? What if Kofman is right when she insists on constantly blurring the line between truth and fiction, life and death? What accounts for the fact that fiction is more uncanny than life, that it is both more unfamiliar and more familiar? What if the literary, the sublime, the imaginary can tell us something true about ourselves, irrespective of the the facts? How would this play itself out for the imaginary and the symbolic? Both Irigaray and Kofman reveal what Gearhart calls "the fundamental complicity of these two orders" (Gearhart 1990, 124). Gearhart shows convincingly how both Freud and Lacan fail to leave room for "more than one scene of sexual difference" (125), while Irigaray, by challenging the "absolute" distinction between the imaginary and the symbolic that Lacan assumes, opens up that space. Irigaray proceeds, in part, by criticizing Freud "for naturalizing the paternal metaphor" (Gearhart 1990, 112). The sense in which Kofman goes one step further than Irigaray when it comes to understanding the mutual implication that pertains between the imaginary and the symbolic lies precisely in Kofman's impacted understanding of Freud's place within the metaphysical tradition.

Before turning, finally, to Kofman's nuanced conception of Freud's role within that history, and thereby back to Kofman's writing of her life, let me briefly rehearse Irigaray's reading of Freud. She says, "There comes, perhaps ineluctably, a moment when she will represent herself as the oppressed, the victim of penile narcissism, just so that she can get possession of those privileges. In a sexual revolt, or revolution that would simply reverse things and risk ensuring an everlasting return of the same. Thus, Freud is to a certain extent right in his opposition to the 'feminists,' except that the reasons he cites are questionable and testify to his failure to grasp the importance of the question" (1985, 119).

If Irigaray avoids any cavalier embrace of feminism, she equally avoids any outright condemnation of Freud, as is clear from her observation that Freud "strikes at least *two blows* at the scene of representation" (1985, 28). An examination of the passage that follows shows that, despite Freud's consistent evaluation of the primacy of the phallus, there is a deeper sense in which he complicates any naive metaphysical conception of presence on which the presence or absence of the phallus would be based. Even if Freud remains a "prisoner of a certain economy of the logos, of a certain logic, notably of 'desire,' whose link to classical philosophy he fails to see," even if he "defines sexual difference as a function of the a priori of the same, having recourse, to support this demonstration, to the age-old processes: analogy, comparison, symmetry, dichotomic oppositions, and so on," and even if "he insists that the sexual pleasure known as masculine is the paradigm for all sexual pleasure," he also makes available certain resources for bringing into question this economy. For, "In order to remain effective, all this certainly needed at the very least to remain hidden!" Freud exhibits a "symptom," and he "offers it up for our analysis," he reveals a "crisis point in metaphysics where we find exposed that sexual 'indifference' that had assured metaphysical coherence and 'closure'" and he therefore offers us a "text . . . to be read," "an ancient dream of self" . . . to be "interpreted" (28).

As an example of the disruption of the usual metaphysical story about presence, a case in point that demonstrates the incursion of the unconscious into the seamless narrative, we might look to the question Irigaray poses to Freud. Does his "discourse . . . necessarily contradic[t] itself when it deals with woman? Since contradiction is the characteristic operation of the unconscious that always inevitably upsets (conscious) discourse when the desire for/of woman is involved? Whence the irrationality of Freud's statement that woman would never be as likely to perform her 'sexual function' as when she is—according to him—a 'little man,' as when she sticks to her primitive, pre-oedipal masculinity" (1985, 110). If everything is determined by Freud's attempt to provide men with resources against their castration anxiety, to shore up masculine desire, to assure the value of the penis, to ward off the threat that woman represents, it would be hardly surprising if various defense mechanisms came into play that blocked or interrupted any coherent narrative Freud might tell concerning women. If Irigaray is right about the the role that women's alleged penis envy plays in conserving the value of the penis, we might be justified in reading Freud's constant protestations that the subject of women is confounding, an enigma, a riddle, a dark continent, as a series of screens or veils hiding the very particular truth that he knows, but disavows—that woman is nothing but a mirror for his own desire.

However compelling Irigaray's narrative, Kofman is correct, I believe, to chide Irigaray for not doing justice to Freud's fractured corpus. I have suggested that Irigaray cannot be accused of simply adopting a dismissive attitude toward Freud, that her reading is, in its own way, a highly nuanced one. Yet, ultimately, Kofman's point must, I think, be granted. There is a sense in which Irigaray oversimplifies Freud, even as she recognizes what it is that drives his various contradictions. The peculiarity of Kofman's critique is that it comes into its own at precisely the point that so many of us have learned so well from Irigaray. That is, it is the sense in which Freud is beholden to the tradition from which he likes to distance himself, the Western philosophical tradition, which Kofman manages to communicate. Kofman says,

> The family romance in which Freud turns literature into the infancy of psychoanalysis is not, however, his own personal fiction. It repeats the fiction invented by western metaphysics as a whole. Freud's gesture is related to the gesture of mastery which is symptomatic of philosophy, and a gesture Aristotle inaugurated by making myth the infancy of philosophy. . . . By distinguishing what Freud *does* from what he *says*, we can see that his texts do indeed lead to the deconstruction of metaphysics. However, these same texts

> concur with the texts of the whole of philosophical tradition and can, genealogically speaking, be classified as *philosophical*. . . . Freudian interpretations involve the same notion of "effect" as philosophy: the "effect" is precisely what philosophy claims to reduce or to dispense with. (1991, 8)

Freud, then, turns out to be more, not less, philosophical than the philosophers! Yet the way in which he is a true philosopher results in the most unphilosophical result. It results in what the philosopher tries (unsuccessfully) to remainder. In just the same way that Freud tells a story about civilization that justifies and normalizes heterosexuality, while rendering primitive and bestial homosexuality, he posits literature as an immature form of writing, apparently unaware of the literary sophistication of his own texts, which, in an irony that would not be lost on Freud, is afforded in no small part by the strategies he engages to keep himself in the dark about his own naïveté concerning women, mothers, and homosexuals, not to mention his own Jewishness.

What, then, is at stake here? Nothing other than the capacity to imagine, to envisage otherwise the conceptual system by which we think. Nothing other than the unconscious, symbolic forces that shape the imaginary of which the West has proved itself capable. That imaginary has been systematic, replete with all the idealism that it can muster. And it has developed at a cost. Castration, femininity, Jewishness, and homosexuality have been among its casualties and its facilitators. Of course, men are no more assured of the phallus than women are. In fact, at least to some extent, their deprivation is all the more worrisome in that it puts them in the rather untenable position of looking to women for confirmation of the phallus that they do not have. As Gearhart puts it, castration figures as a "fundamental lack" that "affects both the masculine and the feminine roles" (1990, 114). Women affirm men's phallic power through their penis envy.

If we take this on board in returning to Dora's case, it is no accident that the tracks along which Freud's thoughts run, the current that flows through his work on femininity and homosexuality, are preordained to meet the requirements of penis envy, as Kofman shows us so clearly.[42] The fact that Freud is blind to Dora's homosexual desire has everything to do with his own symbolic position as analyst, with his own countertransference. So any attempt to uncover the complexities of Dora's case must also confront the imaginary borders within which Freud's discussion—and disclaimers—is confined. If those borders are found to be arbitrarily or artificially constrained by an unreflective homophobia—however much this failure to reflect is a symptom of society in general—they must be contested. And yet, a straightforward contest of wills is one that not only repeats the terms of the problem, but also one that admits defeat in advance.

Concluding Remarks

Like Freud, Kofman put off letting go of a text that was most revelatory of her private being. Like Freud, the text concerns issues surrounding the death of a father, and the desire for a mother. Like Freud, Kofman's text exhibits anxiety about the issue of homosexuality. Finally, like Freud, issues of passing preoccupied Kofman. In Freud's case, his wish was to pass as a respectable doctor, to convert his "poor Jewish" origins into the credentials of science. In Kofman's case, her passing as Mémé's Christian daughter, which began as an adherence to the law of her father, the Judaic taboos of the rabbi, also became a way of returning to her birth mother, but not without a detour, a sexual diversion. Her passing as a Christian daughter made Kofman flush: the proximity of her substitute mother was a cause of homosexual anxiety for Kofman. The issues of passing did not subside for Kofman, although they might have been transformed. In her later life, in her embattled position as a French, female academic, Kofman wanted to pass muster, wanted recognition from a male-dominated academy. She wanted respect.[43] If Freud tried to command respect for his work by adopting, albeit hedged with caveats, and unconvincingly, the badge of science, Kofman mobilized the masks of academic rigor, of fidelity to the texts of the masters (Freud, Nietzsche). If in *Rue Ordener, rue Labat* she allowed such masks to be seen for what they were, she also facilitated a certain breakthrough in her writing.

If originary repression, if castration, is intimately linked to the enigma of femininity, that enigma also founds an enigmatic writing of being Jewish and homosexual. Kofman's writing on Freud draws out, without reducing to one another, the ways in which the enigmas of the Jew, the homosexual, and the woman fold upon and within one another in his work. At the same time, Kofman breathes new life into these enigmas, tracing their intricate relations to one another within her own texts, in her own way, and in the process confounding any attempt to render them entirely separable from one another, and belying the attempt to found one as grounding the other. In the same way, the motif of fire/desire/homosexuality is inseparable from that of water, of micturation, or of the attempt to put out, to control, the fire. Where there is smoke, there is fire; and where there is a castration complex, there is a phallus.

We have seen that Kofman returns to her earlier texts, and rewrites them, sometimes quite literally, in her later texts, rereading and reviewing them, recasting them. The question I conclude with, then, is this: whether it is not precisely Kofman's mastery of texts—a skill she develops early on—her ability to mimic the traditional philosophical game, we might say, the care she takes to see the complexity of the works she reads, that blinds her to the force of Irigaray's point about homosexuality: and whether it is not when she allows that mastery to subside, to unravel into a playful, provocative, captivating, poetic, nonidyllic prose, when she relinquishes control, when she allows herself to be carried away, when the force of her unconscious is unleashed, when she allows the ink of her pen to flow untrammeled, that she relieves herself of the burden, not of urine, but of scholarship (and are they after all, so different?).[44] The ink of a fountain pen that flows as Kofman writes, writes, writes, and the micturation of Freud's primitive male? The quenching of fires must be put away, like toys we weary of in our maturity, as we strive for the higher things of culture, at least according to Freud. Perhaps the same can be said of the game of masterful writing. When Kofman, in her last years, begins to play with fire, she does not allow the smoke to clear, as she relinquishes a certain mastery.[45] Does she not, thereby, in her later texts, open up a more profound but always unspoken communication between her texts and those of Irigaray, from whom we have also learned so well that even Freud's homosexual women could only be homosexual men? For what is at stake in Kofman's conceptual mastery of the labyrinthine and embattled standoff between the imaginary and the symbolic is no small thing. The fantasy of mastery is exposed. Here, surely, is one place where the unity, the mastery, and the totalizing strategy that enhance Kofman's scholarship give way to a poetic gesture that must still, always, like all writing, be compromised, but that also opens onto a future that is no less implicated in a tortured relation to theory than Kofman's own infinite subtlety is implicated in her final desire to let go. Life and death. In Kofman's later texts, in her autobiographical accounts of life and death, Kofman's writing becomes an art, dramatizing the infinite tension between eros and the death drive with which all her work is preoccupied, reveling in the proximity of fiction to reality, staging not the question "Am I a man or a woman?" but another question—through a confrontation of her father's death, a confrontation, which, far from writing out the mother, doubles the mother, through a substitution, an uncanny doubling, of her own mother. How artful is Kofman's writing of this enigma into her final works, and how unconscious it is, remains undetermined. The question Kofman finally asks is: whom do I love? This question neither Freud nor Lacan had the symbolic strength—lacking perhaps, the imagination—to sustain so directly, so elliptically, so enigmatically.

Notes

1. In "Fragment of an Analysis of a Case of Hysteria," Freud writes, "We surely ought not to forget that the perversion which is the most repellent to us, the sensual love of a man for a man, was not only tolerated by a people so far our superiors in cultivation as were the Greeks, but was actually entrusted by them with important social functions" (1905a, 50). It is not clear that Freud follows through on his own advice. He

does seem to forget precisely the possibility that one can both be cultivated and homosexual. If, unlike Freud himself, we take into account his own advice about respecting the different attitudes toward homosexuality across the epochs, we have to be extremely careful about endorsing what our particular era might regard as normal, especially bearing in mind the level of "cultivation" achieved by the Greeks. It is as if Freud makes the mistake of equating homosexuality with an earlier infantile stage, both in terms of individual and societal development, so that homosexuality figures in his account only as that which must be overcome, sublated—or, to employ a more Freudian and less Hegelian turn of phrase, sublimated. It will become evident that women, who, according to Freud's well-known dictum, have inferior powers of sublimation to men, will by the same token not only be able to overcome homosexual desires less easily, but do not even have the physical apparatus to render temptation feasible. This, in turn, will have its impact on women's ostensibly inferior superego, and therefore on the series of related claims Freud makes about women's inclination toward jealousy and envy, and in general women's moral inferiority.

2. Kofman discusses the dream Freud has about his father getting drunk and giving birth to Freud—a dream in which he did not have the "the strength to postpone the satisfaction of his own desires" (1985a, 26). Freud is "heroic" where is father failed.

3. See, for example, Freud 1905a, and Freud 1920, 147–72.

4. Kofman is quoting Freud 1905b, 145–46 n. 1. She quotes the same passage at Kofman 1985a, 146–47.

5. See Freud 1920, 151.

6. It hardly needs to be added that if, in the present days of overpopulation, poverty, famine, and AIDS-ravaged countries, Freud's Darwin-inspired concern to preserve the species seems inapplicable, to say the least.

7. Kofman says, for example, that "Freud knows that in spite of having a poor Jew for a father (whom he replaces in a dream by the professor Meynert, thanks to whom Freud, had he been the professor's son, would have advanced more rapidly), indeed thanks to his own—Jewish—tenacity, he will succeed in the end" (1985a, 25). Elsewhere, Kofman says that "Freud seizes upon the mask of science and of its authority: the only guarantee of infallible success. Even more so because he is only a poor Jew whose speculations no one would give any credit to unless they were covered with the illustrious name of science" (1994a, 99). She then quotes Freud's text "The Future Prospects of Psycho-analytic Theory": "When I assured my patients that I knew how to relieve them permanently of their sufferings they looked around my humble abode, reflected on my lack of fame and title, and regarded me like the possessor of an infallible system at a gambling resort, of whom people say that if he could do what he professes he would look very different himself" (Kofman 1994a, 99–100). Later in the same essay Kofman adds, "A poor Jew who has the audacity to aspire to become a great man, or at least to go further than his father, must not expect to see his way clear after making the first step. All his steps must be difficult, must be costly. And yet he would so much have liked not to pay!" (119).

8. These issues include the contested account Freud provides of the retarded development of the feminine superego and women's alleged incapacity for effective sublimation. Kofman reiterates that one of the most controversial points in Freud for feminists is his conviction that the superego is less well developed in women than it is in men (1985a, 12–13). By implication, the question of the superego relates to how things stand with the imaginary/symbolic divide with regard to the phallus, whether women can preempt the alternative of becoming token men (phallic mothers) or asocial, hysterics or psychotics; the status of the preoedipal, and how far it is useful to routinely and systematically assume its disruptive relation to the oedipal; the possibility of creating a meaningful sense in which women could attain subjectivity that is neither just a replica of, nor just a reactive response to, a preceding masculine version of subjectivity.

9. On this point, see Gearhart 1990.

10. Miep Gies (1987). Ann Smock also comments on how common such occurrences were (see Kofman 1996, xi).

11. Kofman says that school "was the only place where I felt 'myself.' There, I could just manage to stand being separated from my mother. Otherwise I spent my time crying and refused to eat, especially pork, which had always been forbidden me. This refusal, whose pretext was obedience to my father's law, must also have served, without my being completely aware of it, as a means of returning to my mother" (1996, 24).

12. Although Kofman does not refer to Levinas in *Smothered Words*, Blanchot is very much in evidence throughout the text.

13. The phrase "relation without relation" often occurs in the work of Emmanuel Levinas, and is another way of expressing the face-to-face relation—that is, a relation whose bond is prior to its separate terms.

14. Blanchot writes as the final line to "After the Fact," "A story? No. No stories, never again." The essay is written as the afterword to *Vicious Circles* (comprising "The Idyll" [1935] and "The Last Word" [1935–36]). See Blanchot 1999, 199.

15. Compare Madeleine Dobie, who asks in her introduction, "whether, by ending on an affirmation of a new ethics or humanism, *Smothered Words* does not fall short of its own demand by entering into a dialectization of the Shoah which produces an ethical result?" (Kofman 1998b, xix).

16. See both Kofman's discussion of *Unheimlichkeit* in *Lectures de Derrida* (1984), and her discussion of Freud's essay "The Uncanny," on Hoffmann's "The Sandman," in Kofman 1991.

17. In *Enigma*, Kofman discusses at some length Freud's similarity not only to Oedipus but also to Leonardo da Vinci. Unlike Oedipus, and like Leonardo, Freud "does not push on to that impossible goal, does not pursue his investigation to the very end; female sexuality is the 'bedrock,' the limit that analysis as a whole encounters precisely because of the taboo against incest. To respond 'truly' to the riddle of female sexuality would have been to commit incest" (1985a, 94). But Freud "cared too much for

his mother . . . to run the risk of causing her death [Jocasta hangs herself], because he was too conscious also of that risk to be a true hero (Oedipus was unconscious)" (Kofman 1985a, 94). So he gives "false solutions that camouflage the mother's sex, conceal what he has always known" (95). "'Penis envy' is one of these 'screen solutions' that serve as a cover-up" (95). Out of "fear of incest . . . Freud hesitated to publish his writings on the subject of female sexuality" (95). Like Oedipus, the task of the psychoanalyst is to solve the riddle, to unveil, "to bring to light something that has been concealed because of a sexual taboo" (95). "The feminine riddle is the paradigm of every riddle" (96). Freud "sublimated his incestuous desire into a desire for sexual research," but he leaves the "feminine riddle *intact*" (97). But, Kofman adds, it was "[n]ot without toying with it a good deal, not without first conducting, like Oedipus and armed with his Oedipus complex, an investigation that could only be turned back against him, could only lead him off onto a siding, a dead end, that of speculation" (97). Perhaps, in the end, it is not female sexuality as such, but homosexuality, that constitutes the bedrock or limit of Freud's analysis. And of Kofman's, although in a different way.

18. Kofman says "The bad breast in place of the good, the one utterly separate from the other, the one changing into the other" (1996, 66). The section in which this sentence occurs, section 20, is entitled "The Lady Vanishes," also the title of Hitchcock's film. In fact this entire section is repeated verbatim from an earlier essay that Kofman includes in Kofman 1995a, called "Angoisse et catharsis ou comment l'angoisse naît et disparaît (à propos de *The Lady Vanishes*, d'Alfred Hitchcock" (Anxiety and Catharsis, or How Anxiety Was Born and Disappeared [Concerning Hitchcock's *The Lady Vanishes*]). In that essay, which Kofman reads as presenting a ritual initiation into "maternal ambivalence" (Kofman 1995a, 142), in which the bad breast replaces the good, an elderly motherly figure (Miss Froy) disappears, and is replaced, by conspirators, with another woman whose aspect is dour and menacing. In fact, the "good mother" turns out to be a spy—even if, as Kofman points out (and the equivalence between the two women in Hitchcock's film, on the one hand, and Mémé and Kofman's birth mother, on the other hand, is hereby further underscored) she turns out to be a spy for the right side, an English woman whose espionage is directed against the Nazis. Given the point at which Kofman situates this reproduced text in *Rue Ordener, rue Labat*, between the section on Leonardo's "two mothers" (itself a passage reproduced from another text), and the "Idyll," the time in which Kofman enjoys a forbidden—prohibited by the law—and "idyllic" (albeit temporary) reunion with her substitute mother, it seems clear that Kofman's reference to Klein (Kofman 1995a, 142) is far from gratuitous. Kofman is exploring the sense in which Mémé played the role (unwittingly or not) of the father she had lost, producing the distance necessary for Kofman to separate from her birth mother. And yet, Mémé, taking the place of the third party, the father, playing the function of the one to whom the child must turn in order to separate from the father, is a woman. The implication is that Kofman's oedipal trajectory is inhibited by this loving relation with the ambivalent maternal/paternal figure (who plays, perhaps, the role of what Freud calls the father of individual pre-

history, the figure Kristeva makes so much of in her work), a mother who replaces the paternal father, and thereby, perhaps, "interferes" with Kofman's heterosexual "destiny." Kofman playfully puts into question, with her writing of the maternal substitute, the normativity of Freud's heterosexual oedipal scenario.

19. There are parallels between the purse that Kofman mentions here and the jewel case in Dora's first dream (Freud 1905a, 72).

20. Ann Smock writes of Kofman in the introduction to *Smothered Words*, "In an interview, she states that for her *Smothered Words* marked a watershed after which she was no longer able to write in the language of mastery" (Kofman 1998b, xiv).

21. Recall the admonition Kofman's father gave to her mother to look after the baby—Kofman's younger sibling. All Kofman recalls about the card here are the cigarettes (although she remembers earlier the admonition) that she used to procure for her father.

22. It is worth noting that Antelme describes the state of the deportees in terms of their being "drunk," as Kofman observes, "because of the disastrous state of bodies that could do no more than belch up a wretched bile of speech, vomit a stream of the most ignoble words" (Kofman 1998b, 50).

23. This last phrase Kofman quotes from Antelme 1992, 188.

24. See Rose 1990, 128–48. See Cixous and Gearhart, also in Bernheimer and Kahane 1990.

25. See Freud 1905a, 13 n. 1; Freud also put off publishing the text for several years: "I have waited for four whole years since the end of the treatment and have postponed publication till hearing that a change has taken place in the patient's life of such a character as allows me to suppose that her own interest in the occurrences and psychological events which are to be related here may have grown faint" (8).

26. Kofman, "The Double Is/And the Devil: The Uncanniness of *The Sandman* (*Der Sandmann*)," in Kofman 1991, 119–62. Kofman gives a reading of Freud's text "The Uncanny," which refers to Hoffmann 1982.

27. As Gearhart says, "[O]ne aspect of Dora's version of her family history is never scrutinized, although it is duly noted by Freud. . . . 'Dora,' writes Freud, 'looked down on her mother and used to criticize her mercilessly, and she had withdrawn completely from her mother's influence' [Freud 1905a, 20]. Dora's opinion of her mother and her interpretation of their relationship differ insignificantly from Freud's own view, but unlike the rest of her story, the 'truth,' of this assertion will not be scrutinized for its value as an 'alibi'" (1990, 120).

28. In support of Kofman's point (although she does not cite the passage), Hoffman's story is inwardly fractured in a way that Freud does not take up. Freud focuses on the ambivalence of the uncanniness (see Freud 1919, 226), and takes as his starting point Jentsch's observation that "constructed dolls and automata" furnish us with examples of the uncanny because of doubts as to whether "'an apparently animate being is really alive; or conversely, whether a lifeless object might not be in fact animate'" (Freud 1919, 226). But Freud goes on to say of Hoffmann's "The Sandman," "I cannot

think—and I hope most readers of the story will agree with me—that the theme of the doll Olympia, who is to all appearances a living being, is by any means the only, or indeed the most important, element that must be held responsible for the quite unparalleled atmosphere of uncanniness evoked by the story" (227). He goes on to read the story as an expression of Nathaniel's castration anxiety, in which "the figures of his father and Coppelius represent the two opposites into which the father-imago is split by his ambivalence; whereas the one threatens to blind him—that is, to castrate him—the other, the 'good' father, intercedes for his sight" (232 n. 1). At the same time, conserving Jentsch's insight, Freud says that Hoffmann "leaves us in doubt whether what we are witnessing is the first delirium of the panic-stricken boy, or a succession of events which are to be regarded in the story as being real" (228). But Freud's contention that Hoffmann leaves us in doubt completely ignores Nathaniel's mother's persistent unease whenever Coppelius is about to arrive, and more particularly it leaves out of account this passage, which suggests that Nathaniel was not deluded—or, at the very least, that if he was, then his mother shared his delusion: "Of all that concerned Coppelius his mother was told nothing, for they knew she could not think of him without dread because, like Nathaniel, she held him responsible for the death of her husband" (Hoffmann 1982, 108).

29. Hoffmann writes: "I saw that what I had for so long taken to be a wall-cupboard was, rather, a black cavern, in which there stood a small hearth. Coppelius approached it and a blue flame flickered upon the hearth. All kinds of strange implements lay around. Good God! As my father bent down to the fire, he looked quite different! A dreadful convulsive pain seemed to have distorted his gentle, honest features into a repulsive devil mask. He looked like Coppelius. The latter seized the glowing tongs and with them drew brightly glowing substances out of the thick black smoke and began vigorously to hammer away at them. I seemed to see human faces appearing all around, but without eyes—instead of eyes there were hideous black cavities. 'Eyes, bring eyes!' Coppelius cried in a dull, hollow voice. Gripped by wild terror, I screamed aloud and fell out of my hiding place onto the floor" (1982, 90–91). Kofman (1991, 149–50) quotes this after commenting: "The activities Nathaniel's father carries out with Coppelius the lawyer, the sandman, are magical acts of sorcery in which fire and alchemical transformations play an important role" (145). As we just saw, his face becomes a "devil mask," and these "changes in the father's appearance give rise to doubts about paternal identity: is he good? Is he bad? But also, is he active? Is he passive? Man or woman? . . . For Freud the doublings of the father figure stem from the son's ambivalence towards his father, giving birth simultaneously to the devil and the good lord" (155–56). If there is a paternal doubling, there is also a maternal doubling, although, as Kofman says, Freud neglects the figure of the mother.

30. Kofman notices this logic in *Enigma*, where she points out that female analysts are granted the role of confirming Freud's suspicions.

31. See, for example, Freud 1923, esp. chap. 3, and the discussion of conscience in Freud 1919, 235–36. Also see Irigaray 1985, 81, 85–86, 88–90.

32. See, e.g., Freud 1925, 252.

33. Freud says, "As always where the libido is concerned, man has shown himself incapable of giving up a satisfaction he had once enjoyed" (1914, 94). Freud makes a similar point in "Civilization and Its Discontents" when he says that "fundamentally things remain as they were at the beginning" (1930, 72). See also Freud 1918b, 199, on which Kofman comments (see Kofman 1985a, 68).

34. See Freud 1932.

35. Kofman reiterates that one of the most controversial points in Freud for feminists is his conviction that the superego is less well developed in women than it is in men (see Kofman 1985a, 12–13).

36. On the problem of primary narcissism, see Freud 1914, 88. Also see Kofman 1985a, 57–59.

37. See Cixous's 1991 play on the myth of Prometheus.

38. See Gearhart, who points out that when it comes to the role of the mother, Freud abandons his general rule, and takes Dora's derogatory judgments of her mother at face value (1990, 120).

39. On this point see also Freud 1923.

40. See Butler 1997, 119, for a discussion that is clearly indebted to Freud's point here.

41. Laplanche and Pontalis express some skepticism about the clarity of Freud's own insight into the development of his ideas on the referentiality of fantasies, commenting that "a careful study of Freud's concepts and their evolution between 1895 and 1900 reveals that his own—extremely schematic—account does not take into consideration the complexity and depth of his views on phantasy" (1973, 318 n. α). Extrapolating from their point, one could add that, while Freud in fact developed a vocabulary surrounding the imaginary that proved crucial for feminist appropriations of it, he himself was unclear about its etiology. One might say that he blew thick clouds of smoke, creating a fog that has yet to completely clear. Gearhart and Kristeva help to clear it. The claim that desire is in the symbolic realm has to be modified in the direction of Irigaray's and Kofman's recognition of the intricate interrelationship between the symbolic and the imaginary (see Gearhart 1990, 110). Kristeva recognizes that Freud saw the "interdependence" of the different psychic levels at which fantasy operates. It is not merely biological, nor merely a matter of symbolic formation; rather, it is heterogeneous. Like Kofman and Irigaray, Kristeva (1984) sees that the imaginary is thoroughly implicated in the symbolic and the real.

42. In the light of my investigation of the significance of the fire/water motif in Freud's work, it could be shown, even by a cursory examination of his style, that his language is infused with references to currents, streams, and flows, currents that stand in metaphorically for urinating, for homosexual feeling, for bed-wetting, and for masturbation (all of which are linked: see Freud 1905a, 74). "A stream of water which meets with an obstacle in the river-bed is dammed up and flows back into old channels which had formerly seemed fated to run dry" says Freud (51). Or, "[I]n favorable

circumstances, the homosexual current of feeling often runs completely dry . . . I have never yet come through a single psychoanalysis of a man or a woman without having to take into account a very considerable current of homosexuality" (60). Or again, "My powers of interpretation had run dry that day" (59).

43. Despite Kofman's enormously impressive publication record she struggled throughout her life to gain recognition from the French Academy, and was never granted respect in the form of a full professorship.

44. "Idyll, from the Greek ειδωλλιον, the diminutive of ειδωζ, meaning *form*: a small form, a small piece. . . . *Idyll*, the inseparability of form and content" says Kofman (1998b, 23; 1987c, 23).

45. Kofman is particularly interested in the fact that although Freud, like Nietzsche, recognizes the "irreplaceable character of myth," that myth is "the source of all truth" (1985a, 77), like Aristotle he acknowledges its peculiar truth "the better to master it" (77). Myth might have "anticipated" psychoanalysis, but it has been superseded by a higher form of knowledge. For Freud, Kofman says, "myth indeed 'knows,' but its way of knowing is halting, childlike, confused, imagistic, inarticulate, unconscious, and it has to be heightened by—and seen in the light of—adult analytic knowledge in order to accede, *properly speaking*, to Truth" (77–78).

CHAPTER 7

Becoming: *Devenir-femme* in the Work of Sarah Kofman

PENELOPE DEUTSCHER

Becoming I

Auguste Comte's bad style, particularly in his *Cours de philosophie positive*, fascinates Sarah Kofman, as seen in her interpretation of the nineteenth-century positivist philosopher in *Aberrations: Le devenir-femme d'Auguste Comte*. His writing is long, technical, arduous. He does not want to gratify the reader and seems to make a special effort to put us off—"Aucun texte dans toute l'histoire de la philosophie n'est peut-être aussi rébarbatif que celui-là" (Kofman 1978, 11). [Perhaps no text in the history of philosophy is as rebarbative as this one.]

Surprisingly, Kofman describes this deliberate adoption of a technical and arduous style as Comte's becoming-woman (15). Having offered that reading, Kofman also mentions a second phase in Comte's philosophical production, the publication of his *Système de politique positive*. Here Comte reversed his approach, writing in a highly crafted literary style to whose form he pays considerable attention. Kofman suggests that the *Système*, and the outline he provided in his *Synthèse subjective*, can be thought of as an alternative project for how to become woman. Comte's later version involves elaborate rules for writing that constitute, Kofman argues, an alternative means for a male writer to *devenir-femme*. She summarizes, for example, his account of how to achieve, as a philosophical writer, something close to the perfection of some forms of poetry. No sentence should be longer than two lines of manuscript, no paragraph longer than seven sentences. There shall be no hiatus between two phrases, nor between two paragraphs. Unless minor, the same word should not be used in the same sentence, nor in two connecting sentences (Kofman 1978, 241).[1] As Kofman notes, in his *Synthèse subjective* Comte went on explain that philosophical composition could follow the rules of poetic composition, and that the difference between poetic and philosophical volumes was more apparent than real, providing guidelines for suppressing the difference.[2] With this declaration, his ideals for composition had become highly complex. Each volume should normally be divided into seven chapters, each consisting of three parts, again divided into seven sections, each should have seven groups of sentences, and further precisions of this kind followed (Kofman 1978, 242).[3] In this way, Comte suggested the rules for composition would approximate a kind of poetic regularity, as in the case, he said, of the great poems (*les grands poèmes*) having the form of thirteen songs (*chants*), broken into parts, sections and groups.[4]

Kofman locates forms of a Comtean becoming-woman both in a philosophical style carefully composed to be like a form of poetry, and in a philosophical style so devoid of literary artifice that it seems designed to repel the reader.

Becoming II

Becoming and becoming-woman are two of the most constant and operative concepts in Sarah Kofman's work. At one point, becoming-woman is associated with what she confusingly refers to as bisexuality—"[O]n ne tient pas comte de la bisexualité. On peut toujours écrire comme l'autre sexe" (Kofman 1998a, 185–86). [We don't take bisexuality into account: one can always write like the opposite sex.] According to this idea of bisexuality, many or all of us have the capacity to take on aspects or styles of, identifications or syntheses with, the opposite sex.

Kofman's comment about bisexuality refers to a work to which Kofman had dedicated an essay in her collection *Séductions: De Sartre à Héraclite*. As she explains responding to an interview question about l'écriture féminine: "Il y a une écriture qu'on pourrait qualifier de féminine, mais certains hommes peuvent écrire aussi de cette manière-là . . . Diderot, homme, a écrit ce texte qui est censé être les mémoires d'une femme" (Kofman 1998a, 185). [There is a kind of writing one can describe as feminine, but some men can also write in that way . . . Diderot, a man, wrote this text which was supposed to be the memoirs of a woman.]

Kofman's comment about Diderot implies that becoming the opposite sex is a project in which any of us can engage. Many writers can write in a feminine manner, for example. But in her discussions of the concept of becoming-woman, resemblance, or making a reader or observer think one belongs to the opposite sex, is not what Kofman means by becoming-woman. She is interested, for example, in the phenomenon whereby specifics of childhood history and one's psychic makeup lead to some subjects having an adult, unconscious identificatory relationship with women and femininity. In this sense, becoming-woman could still be seen as a creative project, but not a deliberate or consciously authored project. It is not, in this context, Kofman's view that any man—or woman—can arbitrarily engage in that process in a successful or significant way, adopting and then relinquishing sexes as one pleases. Instead, she considers the psychic makeup of our identification with masculinity or femininity to be a kind of fatality: "Ce destin n'est pas un choix. Il est tributaire de l'histoire de l'individu, de ses rapports avec ses relations, etc." (Kofman 1998a, 177). [This destiny isn't a choice. It is tributary to an individual's history, one's relationships with one's relations, etc.] In this sense Kofman analyzes identification with women to be found in the cases of Freud (Kofman 1985a), Auguste Comte (Kofman 1978), and Jean-Jacques Rousseau (Kofman 1982), interpreting these identifications as types of becoming-women.

Being women or men involves processes of becoming, yet this does not imply volitional nor easy transformation. As Kofman notes, Beauvoir thought that women were coerced into becoming women. While the necessity for coercion implies the risk of becoming otherwise, strong forces ensure that women do become women, according to social norms. Nonetheless, Kofman does think that transformation is importantly connected to the notion of becoming, and she develops this at one point by reference to transsexualism, interpreted by her as yet another possibility for becoming otherwise.

Kofman concludes the interview in which she discusses Beauvoir, Diderot's *The Nun*, and the importance of becoming with the non sequitur, "Maintenant on commence à reconnaître les transsexuels" (Kofman 1998a, 186) [Today, we're starting to acknowledge transsexuals], attaching this to the bland observation, "La catégorisation en deux sexes est purement sociale" (186) [Categorization into two sexes is purely social]. Perhaps Kofman is reiterating a trajectory inspired by Robert Stoller, a trajectory that connected transsexualism with the conceptual separation between sex and gender and with a concept of male and female behavior as acquired, social and mutable.[5] Kofman does take transsexualism to demonstrate that femininity is not the inevitable result of being a woman. However, it does not indicate that the permutations of femininity and masculinity are arbitrary.[6] Certainly, the significance of transsexualism is vague in Kofman's work, but she takes it to be the emblem of possible transformation. She confuses things further by drawing a comparison between her own work, her own understanding of becoming, and the concept of becoming in the work of Beauvoir. Beauvoir uses the verb *devenir* to remind readers that one is not born a woman—one becomes one.[7] In fact, the broad interest of Kofman's career is in the becoming-women of men, and particularly of male philosophers. But discussing Beauvoir's work, Kofman associates her own project with Beauvoir's demonstration that women must become women.

The notion of becoming changes again. Briefly, it is connected to the kind of social constructionism with which Beauvoir's work is sometimes associated.

Here is Kofman commenting on the notion of becoming in the context of Beauvoir's work: "La femme telle qu'on se la représente, comme sexe faible, comme deuxième sexe, est le résultat d'un devenir-femme au cours de l'histoire" (Kofman 1998a, 176). [Woman, as she has been represented throughout history, as the weaker sex, the second sex, is the result of a becoming-woman throughout the course of history.] Quite simply, as she defines it, Beauvoir's "'on ne naît pas femme, on le devient' [one is not born woman, but rather one becomes, a woman] is a nonessentialist (*non essentialiste*) conception of the human and of woman" (see Kofman 1998a, 177). Kofman seems to take Beauvoir's view to be that, as she also says, our "categorization into two sexes is purely social" (Kofman 1998a, 186). She claims that the notion of becoming that proved to be so important throughout her work is indebted to Beauvoir.[8]

If the references to fatality and destiny do not sit especially well with the idea that any of us could write like the opposite sex, neither do either of these ideas (both associated with the notion of becoming) sit especially well with the references to Beauvoir. Kofman's mobilization of a concept of becoming is, however, easier to follow as she deploys it, and I turn now to the examples of the becoming-woman of Jean-Paul Sartre, Jean-Jacques Rousseau, Sigmund Freud, and Auguste Comte.

Rousseau, Freud, and Sartre

In Kofman's *Le respect des femmes*, becoming-woman is a social and political threat discussed by Jean-Jacques Rousseau. Becoming here represents the very sexual confusion that Rousseau thought jeopardized society, nature, and morality. Resemblance between the sexes is for Rousseau always catastrophic, leading to what he describes as the "mélange désordonné des sexes" (1962, 453) [disordered mixing up of the sexes]. It is the mark of "general perversion, "la perversion générale: le devenir-homme de la femme, le devenir-femme de l'homme, la perte pour chacun des sexes de sa spécificité" (Kofman 1982, 73) [the loss by each of the sexes of its specificity]. Becoming the other sex is, in the Rousseauist context, easily broached, and the resulting collapse of sexual specificity can occur so easily that Rousseau is horrified by the possibilities. The rigidity and commitment to sexual difference in Rousseau's work interconnects with his constant signaling of its fragility. Also, as Kofman points out, the collapse of the one sex drags the collapse of the other with it. The stability of the difference between the two sexes collapses, so little are the sexes immune from each other: "En se perdant, elle perd l'homme avec elle: le devenir-homme de la femme entraîne le devenir-femme de l'homme et la perversion radicale de l'ordre de la nature, de la morale et de la société" (Kofman 1982, 110). [In losing herself, she loses man: the becoming-man of a woman involves the becoming woman of man and the radical perversion of the order of nature, morality, and society.] When woman becomes man through resemblance, man risks losing his specific characteristics (see Kofman 1982, 113). To some extent, woman becomes man by appropriating his public role and civic persona, taking his place (see Kofman 1982, 126.) However, Rousseau qualifies that such women do not truly attain masculinity, instead becoming ridiculous, pretentious figures. While they never succeed in resembling men, they do relinquish their proper place. While women do not gain masculinity, men do lose it—also becoming ridiculous (see Kofman 1982, 126). In Rousseau's world, it seems everyone is a variation on a possible woman, with men so easily ceasing to be men.

There is another sense of becoming woman. Kofman comments on Rousseau's discussion of his lack of success with "you women." Perhaps Rousseau's failure occurs, she says, directly to women: "[P]arce qu'il vous ressemble trop? Parce qu'il s'est trop identifié à vous? Être une femme, tel est peut-être la crainte, le désir le plus profond de Rousseau. Non pas une femme frivole, qui écrit, tient la plume ou le pinceau, une femme-homme: cela, Rousseau l'a été. Mais une vraie femme, une mère (Kofman 1982, 146–47). [Because he resembles you too much? Perhaps because he identifies with you too much? Being a woman, perhaps this is Rousseau's fear, and his deepest desire. Not a frivolous woman, who writes, deploys pen or paintbrush, a woman-man: Rousseau has been all of this. But a real woman, a mother.] She mentions, speculatively, that late in life Rousseau took to wearing long Armenian robes, which "le travestissait en femme" (147). Similarly, along these lines, Kofman wonders if Rousseau's urinary disorder, placed in the context of having been told that women give birth to children by urination, is again a manifestation of his identification with his mother, a trauma about and identification with the maternal role (see Kofman 1982, 149).

On the one hand, Rousseau becomes woman; on the other, he writes about the social problem of becoming woman. Kofman frequently interprets the identification of male authors with a feminine and usually a maternal figure, quite often maternal figures in their own lives. Kofman also proposes that Freud and Sartre identified with maternal figures, and with their own mothers. In Freud's work, this is again interconnected with the problem of becoming, a concept she locates in his work, as when she writes of Freud, "[O]ne may well ask how masculine bisexuality is manifested. It is true that Freud does not inquire into the little's boy's becoming-man" (Kofman 1985a, 150; translation modified). Introducing the notion of original bisexuality, Freud declares that all of us have elements of femininity, sexually indistinguishable tendencies toward activity and passivity, and sexually indistinguishable choices of love object. Kofman speculates that Freud uses the concept of original bisexuality to flatter women—for example, women psychoanalysts who learn from Freud they are more masculine than feminine. He discusses the problem of women's becoming women, but not the problem of man's becoming man, and he shows a great deal more alacrity in showing the masculinity of some women than in theorizing the femininity of men—and, indeed, of himself. Kofman comments, "[T]he thesis of bisexuality thus implies that Sigmund Freud himself could not have been *purely and simply* a man (*vir*) . . . Freud never appeals to this argument in his own defense, however, never exhibits his femininity as he indulges in exposing the masculinity of his female colleagues. . . . And it is as though Freud were loudly proclaiming the universality of bisexuality in order better to disguise his silent disavowal of his own femininity, his paranoia" (Kofman 1985a, 15).

On Kofman's reading, Freud's theory of women's penis envy is a blind that deflects attention from his ambivalence about feminine figures as all-powerful (all-powerful both as maternal and as narcissistic, libidinally self-satisfied figures who are loved, rather than loving the other), a power and self-sufficiency he envies and admires. This is so disturbing that Freud covers up this view of women. It is not he that envies women, it is women who envy the penis. So, when Freud attributes men with power and the penis envied by women, this is only as the inverse of the original power he perceives in woman (Kofman 1985a, 85). If, as a man, he does identify with having power, this is also an envious identification with women, and thus, a formation of Freud's becoming-woman (as Kofman uses this concept).

Notice the high degree of variability in the concept of becoming-woman introduced by these various interpretations. To turn to another example, when becoming-woman is identified in the work of Jean-Paul Sartre (Kofman 1990b), Kofman is not describing any kind of resemblance to women, however we might define this, nor Sartre's thinking he is like a woman, or feminine. As Kofman notes, for example, Sartre rejected a style of inflated, autoreferential, self-enclosed prose he took to be bourgeois and feminine (Kofman 1990b, 160), when he explains that by contrast, "I treated my pen as a sword" (Sartre 1967, 157).

Instead, Kofman interrogates Sartre's desire to be remembered by us, as manifested in his autobiography. To understand what becoming-woman is for Sartre, we must know what woman is for Sartre. In the sense in which he importantly becomes woman, woman is that which is engaged in the *fort* and the *da*—the bobbin thrown away and retracted in a staging of the mother who is absent and appears, and whom, above all, we miss. Sartre wants to be missed—as a woman is missed, as he misses women, and his becoming a woman is his attempt to manipulate himself into being a loved and lost, mourned and regretted, remembered love object, whose absence and presence we cannot control (see Kofman 1990b, 166).

Kofman also proposes that Sartre's becoming a woman is a becoming like a mother, so that we might miss him as he misses his mother. But, as with her reading of Rousseau, she offers these kinds of readings without committing to a surface-depth model or positing a psychology or psychic persona behind the text. She insists that she is not trying to psychoanalyze the authors, though she does locate variations on maternal identification in Rousseau, Comte, Sartre, Freud, and many others.

Becoming III

For Kofman to describe the becoming-woman of Freud, Comte, or Rousseau is not to describe their becoming "like" a woman. She does not draw on historical suppositions about women's qualities, such as that to become woman is to become hysterical, emotional, or sensuous. Instead, to become woman is to identify with (or, more directly, again become) parts of what one associates with being a woman. To make the point more clearly, Kofman locates a "becoming-woman" equally in the rationalist, off-putting, dry, scientific prose of Comte, the florid, hysterical flourishes of Rousseau, and the specific theoretical conclusions about women arrived at by Freud. There is nothing similar about the style or manner of these writers. Yet they all, in Kofman's opinion, engage in becoming-woman, not through resemblance to women, but because what they become bears a relation to what they differently associate with women.

Auguste Comte's becoming-woman is located both in his dry, technical writing, and in his visions that philosophy might be like poetry. Writing in the most unseductive way possible is an attempt to deny us access to his system in the way that, he imagines, women deny men access. Again, the point is not one of resemblance. He does not think that women are unseductive, nor that they try to be so. In Kofman's concept of becoming-woman, a subject takes a part for a nonexistent whole, counter to the logic of resemblance. Comte ascribes to women a shameful secret, and having done so, becomes woman by acting in the dissimulating, off-putting way he associates with having a shameful secret (Kofman 1978, 14–15), acting as if one had something to hide. In this sense, the bad style is Comte's protective veil. Comte's becoming-woman can and does take another and opposite form, as when Kofman takes Comte's defense of the "indispensable" subordination of women to be another form of becoming-woman.[9] In this case he is trying to seduce (in other words, to act seductively, like a woman) the reader with these arguments; and he does so because "sous l'effet, peut-être aussi, de la crainte qu'à trop bien défendre les femmes on puisse le soupçonner de s'identifier à elles" (Kofman 1978, 232) [in his fear perhaps also of defending women too well, one might suspect him of identifying with them].

Kofman also locates Comte's becoming-woman in his conception of ideas, associated with the conception of children. She notes that Comte speaks not of his ideas but of his "conceptions" (16); in certain modes of his isolation, since he fears being manipulated like a woman (24); in his fear of madness, since he is worried it will make him act like a woman (279); in his anxious desire for approval (251); in his desire to be made fertile by others by stealing their ideas (24); and in certain of his physical ailments that he associates with pregnancy (26–28). It also appears, she says, in his feminine position in relation to Caroline Massin, his first wife, who took the active, authoritative position in the household, whereas Comte associates femininity with a submissive position; in his relationship to Massin, whom he expected to be a kind of midwife to his ideas; in his interest in regenerating humanity (308); in his teaching position at the Ecole polytechnique, which he judged to be servile, to be menial, and to involve overly long hours; in his constant (as she thinks) guilt about women; and in the way he always seems to be trying to compensate or make up to women for his arguments about their necessary subordination—as when he argues that women are afflicted with a fundamental inferiority but are also endowed with a "secondary" kind of superiority necessary to domestic existence and involving a heartfelt devotion and sweetness of character (233).[10] Finally, we can add to this list Kofman's view that Comte identified with his second love, Clotilde de Vaux, whom he thought awakened him to a second life, as when he writes in a letter to her of 1845, "Mon organisme a reçu d'une très tendre mère certaines cordes intimes, éminemment féminines, qui n'ont pu encore assez vibrer, faute d'avoir été convenablement ébranlées" (Comte 1973–90, 3:78–86, esp. 84). [My whole organism received from a very tender mother certain intimate, eminently feminine harmonies that have never sufficiently vibrated, never having been appropriately shaken up.] Perhaps, she speculates, he has some kind of deposit of femininity from his mother that has been in the silent shadows, until now, when the feminine Clotilde can bring it to life, and enable him to be reconciled with his femininity" (Kofman 1978, 241). At this point we see in Comte's work the change in style noted above by Kofman, in which his project is to write philosophy as poetry. For, she argues:

> [C]hanger de sexe, c'est nécessairement changer de style. Devenir femme donne au moins comme compensation avouée immédiate celle de pouvoir donner du plaisir au lecteur, de créer un commerce véritable avec lui et d'y gagner en échange la reconnaissance et, qui sait, la chaire de mathématiques . . . (Kofman 1978, 241)

> [T]o change one's sex is to change one's style, necessarily. Becoming woman yields at least this avowed and immediate compensation: being able

> to give the reader pleasure, to create a real exchange with him, and to be rewarded in the exchange by his recognition and, who knows, even a chair in mathematics . . .

But when, like his mother, Clotilde dies, the identificatory nature of his relationship with both will lead, Kofman argues, to a melancholic identification with them, a taking of their place, which he depicts in terms of identification and incorporation. He reidentifies with certain religious values, perhaps in an attempt to retrospectively make amends to his mother. After Clotilde's death, Comte gives himself over to a melancholic and ascetic existence: "Comte devient alors femme en s'identifiant à la morte, en l'incorporant, en la dévorant: pour que Clotilde-Rosalie survive" (Kofman 1978, 243). [Comte then becomes woman by identifying with the deceased, incorporating her, devouring her so that Clotilde-Rosalie survive.] On her reading, by identifying with Clotilde and with his mother, Rosalie, he succeeds "à conserver, de façon quasi hallucinatoire la présence de (des) la femme(s) aimée(s)" (243) [in conserving in nearly hallucinatory fashion, the presence of the loved woman, or women].

Transformation

It is far from obvious, in reading these texts on Rousseau, Comte, and Sartre how processes of becoming-woman are transformational projects. While Kofman refers her concept of becoming-woman to Beauvoir, one is hard pressed to find any of Beauvoir's interests in Kofman's depictions of how Sartre, Rousseau, Comte, and Freud become women. Nonetheless, I think Kofman's reference to Beauvoir's project is helpful in clarifying what she considers is being transformed in these processes of becoming. It is not just Rousseau, Comte, Freud, or Sartre, not just the men who become. It is the woman—the woman of the "becoming-woman."

For what has happened to the notion of woman, in the becoming women of Sartre, Rousseau, Freud, and Comte? It is dispersed amongst the diverse and inconsistent resonances of being modest, seductive, frivolous, fertilizable, manipulable, maternal, appropriative of man's place, narcissistically self-sufficient, self-protective, penis envying, bourgeois, missed, mourned, regretted, sickly, mad, degraded, deathlike, stimulating, rejuvenating, moral, tender, figures whose presence and absence one cannot control.

When, to become woman, Comte is by alternation and sometimes at once serious, scientific, dry, technical, seductive, religious, maternal, and mad, the very sequence at once constitutes and destabilizes what being a woman is, emphasizing the contestable nature of this question, its transience, flexibility, and lack of fixity. In Rousseau's texts, it is striking that there are few reference points for a definitive masculinity. Moreover, while there are many variations on becoming-woman, there is also no definitive woman—yet no one quite becomes man. So Kofman's readings lead to a sense of the destabilization and fragmentation of gender difference at the heart of its life as stable, static, and oppositional. As transformational, it opens up sexual difference to a greater sense of its evanescence. Rousseau—to take an example—an author who takes great pains to emphasize the oppositional nature of sex, also describes its elusive nature, and transforms a concept on which he heavily relies. There is a transformation of femininity by the men, the male philosophers, who identify with it.

By contrast to the work of Luce Irigaray, Kofman does not elaborate an alternative concept of sexual difference in place of the notion she destabilized. Yet, according to Kofman, we are all, women no less than men, becoming-woman. As she does not analyze the becoming-woman of women, we have few resources to establish her relation to Beauvoir's becoming-woman. If she is fascinated in the becoming-woman of male philosophers, she also considers this process of becoming-woman to be melancholic, in the sense of an identification that implies refused and incorporated loss—in Judith Butler's words "an object is phantasmatically taken in or on . . . as a way of refusing to let it go." Recall how Butler points out that "drag allegorizes some set of melancholic incorporative fantasies that stabilize *gender*" and compare with Kofman.[11] On Butler's reading one can think of the "strictly straight" woman who identifies with the woman that she loves and won't give up in terms of a preservational melancholia. From Kofman's perspective the truest feminine melancholic is the man most committed to oppositional sexual difference. Whereas a different reading could find it useful to argue that the straight man mimes or cites the man he "never" loved, Kofman searches for the transformational significance of the straight, male philosopher, highly committed to gender opposition, who becomes the women he never was. Though she referenced the work of queer theorist Eve Sedgwick (Kofman 1990b, 42), it may seem that Kofman is not engaged in a queering of these philosophers. The contrast with Sedgwick and Butler might suggest that she radically heterosexualizes these figures, relentlessly reading heterosexual desire back into their work. All these men are enamored of women, and Kofman could have stressed that the disavowal of homosexuality is a means of being the man in place of loving him. Instead, loving women, while they try to hold on to gender opposition, these men are, on her reading, engaged in a process of *becoming* the women, a becoming-woman Kofman argues does take place. In this way, she does, after all, locate a disavowed homosexual love, not of the man for the man, but of the women for the women. The love that does not speak its name is the philosopher men loving the women as they become them.

Notes

Unless otherwise noted, the translations are the author's.

1. "Pour utiliser autant que possible ma sollicitude littéraire, je dois ici caractériser les diverses prescriptions que je me suis graduellement imposées [. . .] Afin d'éviter les phrases trop longues, je n'ai jamais permis qu'aucune excédât deux lignes manuscrites, ou cinq imprimées. L'œil et l'esprit ont obtenu les haltes convenables, en restreignant à sept phrases la plus grande extension de mes alinéas, qui ne sont pas seulement typographiques. Sans que la prose doive aspirer à la perfection musicale de la poésie, je me suis efforcé de l'en rapprocher en m'interdisant tout hiatus, même entre deux phrases ou deux alinéas. J'ai d'ailleurs évité de reproduire un mot quelconque, non seulement envers chaque phrase mais pour deux phrases consécutives, même en changeant d'alinéa; sauf quant aux monosyllabes auxiliaires" (Comte 1851–54c, 10:ix). [To engage as much as possible my literary sensibility, I must here characterize the diverse prescriptions that I have gradually imposed. . . . To avoid phrases that are too long, I have never allowed any to exceed two manuscript lines, or five printed lines. The eye and mind have found suitable pauses, which are not only typographical, when I have limited the most extended of my paragraphs to seven sentences. Without the prose having to aspire to the musical perfection of poetry, I have tried to get closer to it by denying myself any hiatus, even between two sentences or two paragraphs. Moreover I have avoided reproducing any word, not only within each sentence but for two consecutive sentences, even in changing paragraphs, except for auxiliary monosyllables.]

2. Comte 1851–54b, 756, discussed in Kofman 1978, 242.

3. Comte 1851–54b, 755, discussed in Kofman 1978, 242.

4. Comte 1851–54b, 756, discussed in Kofman 1978, 242.

5. See Stoller 1984.

6. In the 1970s, following Stoller's writing, some feminists saw transsexualism as an emblem of the possibility of social change. The point that women could become otherwise gendered, and the lesson that there was nothing about the female or male body that dictated the behavior that had to accompany it, since this was a matter of social forces and behavioral indoctrination, meant gender was open to change through an alteration in environmental factors. For a critical survey of the influence of Stoller on feminist thinking about gender in the 1970s, see the first chapter of Gatens 1996.

7. Famously, at the beginning of the second volume of *Le deuxième sexe*, Beauvoir says, "On ne naît pas femme: on le devient" (Beauvoir 1976, 13). Translated in Beauvoir 1989, 267.

8. Kofman had closely read Beauvoir as a student, and had written about her ethics as an academic.

9. Comte 1830–42, 6:57. Kofman also refers us to Comte's correspondence with John Stuart Mill on the status of women. See, for example, *Lettre à John Stuart Mill du 5 octobre* 1843, in Comte 1973–90, 2:196–203; translated in Comte 1955, 186–94.

10. See Auguste Comte, *Lettre à Valat du 16 novembre, 1825*, in Comte 1973–90, 1:196–203; and see Comte 1830–42, 1:162–68, esp. 167. Also see Comte 1851–54, 7:231–36.

11. See Judith Butler 1997, 146.

References

Antelme, Robert. 1992. *The Human Race.* Trans. J. Haight and Annie Mahler. Evanston, IL: Marlboro Press/Northwestern University Press. Original French edition: *L'espèce humaine*. Paris: Gallimard, 1957.

Arendt, Hannah. 1951. *The Origins of Totalitarianism.* Cleveland: World Publishing Co.

Aschheim, Steven. E. 1992. *The Nietzsche Legacy in Germany. 1890–1990.* Berkeley and Los Angeles: University of California Press.

Bachelard, Gaston. 1968. *The Psychoanalysis of Fire.* Trans. Alan C. M. Ross. Boston: Beacon Press.

Bataille, Georges. 1991. *The Accursed Share, Vols. II and III.* Trans. Robert Hurley. New York: Zone Books.

Beauvoir, Simone de. 1976. *Le deuxième sexe.* Vol. 2. Paris: Gallimard. [1949]. Translated in Beauvoir 1989.

———. 1989. *The Second Sex.* Trans. H. M. Parshley. New York: Vintage. Translation of Beauvoir 1976.

Benjamin, Walter. 1968. *Illuminations.* Ed. H. Arendt. Trans. H. Zohn. New York: Schocken Books.

Bernheimer, Charles and Claire Kahane, eds. 1990. *In Dora's Case: Freud-Hysteric-Feminism.* 2nd ed. Gender and Culture Series, ed. Carolyn G. Heibrun and Nancy K. Miller. New York: Columbia University Press.

Binion, Rudolph. 1968. *Frau Lou: Nietzsche's Wayward Disciple.* Princeton, NJ: Princeton University Press.

Blanchot, Maurice. 1981. *The Madness of the Day.* Trans. Lydia Davis. Barrytown, NY: Station Hill Press.

———. 1999. *The Station Hill Blanchot Reader: Fiction and Literary Essays*, ed. George Quasha. Barrytown, NY: Station Hill Press.

Butler, Judith. 1997. *The Psychic Life of Power: Theories in Subjection.* Stanford, CA: Stanford University Press.

Cixous, Hélène and Catherine Clément. 1990. The Untenable. In Bernheimer and Kahane, 276–93.

———. 1991. *The Book of Promethea.* Trans. Betsy Wing. Lincoln: University of Nebraska Press.

Comte, Auguste. 1830–1842. *Cours de philosophie positive.* Vols 1–6 of *Oeuvres d'Auguste Comte*. Paris: Editions Anthropos.

———. 1851–54a. *Oeuvres d'Auguste Comte.* 12 vols. Paris: Editions Anthropos.

———. 1851–54b. *Synthèse subjective ou Système universel des conceptions propres à l'état normal de l'humanité.* Vol. 12 of Comte 1851–54a.

———. 1851–54c. *Système de politique positive ou traité de sociologie* (in four volumes). Vols. 7–10 of Comte 1851–54a. *Oeuvres d'Auguste Comte* (in twelve volumes). Paris: Editions Anthropos.

———. 1955. *The Correspondence of John Stuart Mill and Auguste Comte.* Trans. Oscar A. Haac. New Brunswick, NJ: Transaction Publishers.

———. 1973–90. *Correspondance générale et confessions.* Paris: Mouton. Partially translated in Comte 1955.

DeArmitt, Pleshette. 2006. Sarah Kofman. *Jewish Women: A Comprehensive Historical Encyclopedia.* Ed. Moshe Shalvi. CD-ROM. Jerusalem: Shalvi Publishing Ltd.

Derrida, Jacques. 1973. La question du style. In *Nietzsche aujourd'hui?* 235–88. Paris: Union Générale d'Éditions. Translated as The Question of Style, Trans. Ruben Berezdivin, In *The New Nietzsche: Contemporary Styles of Interpretation*, ed. David B. Allison, 2nd ed. Cambridge, MA: MIT Press, 1985.

———. 1978. *La vérité en peinture.* Paris: Flammarion. Translated as *The Truth in Painting*, Trans. Geoff Bennington and Ian McLeod. Chicago: University of Chicago Press, 1987.

———. 1985. Otobiographies. Trans. Avital Ronnell. In *The Ear of the Other: Otobiography, Transference, Translation; Texts and Discussions with Jacques Derrida*, ed. Christie V. McDonald. Trans. Peggy Kamuf. New York: Schocken Books.

———. 1995. *On the Name.* Stanford, CA: Stanford University Press.

———. 1997. Untitled. *Sarah Kofman*, ed. Françoise Collin and Françoise Proust, 131–65. Paris: Les Cahiers du Grif, Descartes & Cie.

———. 2001. In *The Work of Mourning*, ed. Pascale-Anne Brault and Michael Naas. Chicago: University of Chicago Press.

———. 2007. Introduction . Trans. Pascale-Anne Brault and Michael Naas. In *Sarah Kofman, Selected Writings.* Eds. Thomas Albrecht with Georgia Albert and Elizabeth G. Rottenberg. Stanford, CA: Stanford University Press

Detienne, Marcel and Jean-Piérre Vernant. 1978. *Cunning Intelligence in Greek Culture and Society.* Trans. Janet Lloyd. Atlantic Highlands, NJ: Humanities Press.

Deutscher, Penelope and Kelly Oliver, eds. 1999. *Enigmas: Essays on Sarah Kofman.* Ithaca, New York and London: Cornell University Press.

Diderot, Denis. 1959. *Œuvres esthétiques.* Ed. Paul Vernière. Paris: Garnier.

Duffy, M. F. and W. Mittelman. 1988. Nietzsche's Attitude toward the Jews. *Journal of the History of Ideas* 49, 2 (April–June): 301–17.

Ernst, M. 1976. *A Week of Kindness: Or the Seven Deadly Elements.* New York: Dover Publications.

Freud, Sigmund. 1905a. Fragment of an Analysis of a Case of Hysteria. In vol. 7 of Freud 1953–66.

———. 1905b. Three Essays on the Theory of Sexuality. In vol. 7 of Freud 1953–66.

———. 1914. On Narcissism: An Introduction. In vol. 14 of Freud 1953–66.

———. 1916. On Transience. In vol. 14 of Freud 1953–66.

———. 1918a. From the History of an Infantile Neurosis. In vol. 17 of Freud 1953–66.

———. 1918b. On the Taboo of Virginity. In vol.11 of Freud 1953–66.

———. 1919. The Uncanny. In vol. 17 of Freud 1953–66.

———. 1920. The Psychogenesis of a Case of Homosexuality in a Woman. In vol. 18 of Freud 1953–66.

———. 1923. The Ego and the Id. In vol. 19 of Freud 1953–66.

———. 1925. Some Psychical Consequences of the Anatomical Distinction between the Sexes. In vol.19 of Freud 1953–66.

———. 1930. Civilization and Its Discontents. In vol. 21 of Freud 1953–66.

———. 1932. The Acquisition and Control of Fire. In vol. 22 of Freud 1953–66.

———. 1940. Medusa's Head. In vol. 18 of Freud 1953–66.

———. 1953–66. *The Standard Edition of the Complete Psychological Works of Sigmund Freud.* Trans. and ed. James Strachey. 24 vols. London: Hogarth Press and Institute of Psychoanalysis.

Gatens, Moira. 1996. *Imaginary Bodies: Ethics, Power and Corporeality.* New York: Routledge.

Gearhart, Suzanne. 1990. The Scene of Psychoanalysis: The Unanswered Questions of Dora. In Bernheimer and Claire Kahane, 105–27.

Gies, Miep and A. L. Gold. 1987. *Anne Frank Remembered: The Story of the Woman who Helped to Hide the Frank Family.* New York: Simon & Schuster.

Hayman, R. 1980. *Nietzsche: A Critical Life.* New York: Penguin Books.

Hesiod. 1943. *Theogony.* Trans. Hugh G. Evelyn-White. Cambridge, MA: Harvard University Press.

Hoffmann, E. T. A. 1982. The Sandman. In *Tales of Hoffmann*, trans. R. J. Hollingdale. Harmondsworth: Penguin Books.

Irigaray, Luce. 1985. *Speculum of the Other Woman.* Trans. G. C. Gill. Ithaca, NY: Cornell University Press.

Kofman, Sarah. 1970. *L'enfance de l'art, une interpretation de l'esthétique freudienne.* Paris: Galilée.

———. 1972. *Nietzsche et la métaphore.* Paris: Payot. A translation of Kofman, 1993b.

———. 1973a. *Camera obscura: De l'idéologie.* Paris: Galilée.

———. 1973b. Un philosophe "unheimlich." In *Écarts: Quatre essais à propos de Jacques Derrida*, ed. Lucette Finas, Sarah Kofman, Roger Laporte, and Jean-Michel Rey. 107–204. Paris: Fayard. Revised in Kofman, *Lectures de Derrida* (Paris: Galilée, 1984), 11–114.

———. 1974. *Quatres romans analytiques.* Paris: Galilée.

———. 1978. *Aberrations: Le devenir-femme d'Auguste Comte.* Paris: Aubier-Flammarion.

———. 1979. *Nietzsche et la scène philosophique.* Paris: Galilée.

———. 1980. *L'énigme de la femme: La femme dans les textes de Freud.* Paris: Galilée. Translated in Kofman 1985a.

———. 1982. *Le respect des femmes (Kant et Rousseau).* Paris: Galilée.

———. 1983a. *Comment s'en sortir?* Paris: Galilée.

———. 1983b. *Un métier impossible.* Paris: Galilée.

———. 1984a. *Autobiogriffures.* Paris: Editions Galilée.

———. 1984b. La ressemblance des portraits (À propos du *Salon de 1767* consacré à *La Tour*). *L'Esprit Créateur* 24, no. 1 (Spring): 13–32.

———. 1985a. *The Enigma of Woman: Woman in Freud's Writings.* Trans. C. Porter. Ithaca, NY: Cornell University Press. A translation of Kofman 1980.

———. 1985b. *Mélancolie de l'art.* Paris: Galilée.

———. 1986a. Autobiographical Writings. Trans. Frances Bartowski. *Substance* 44 (1986): 12. Partial translation of Kofman 1983a.

———. 1986b. *Pourquoi rit-on?* Paris: Galilée.

———. 1987a. *Conversions: "Le marchand de Venise" sous le signe de Saturne.* Paris: Galilée.

———. 1987b. Nietzsche and the Obscurity of Heraclitus. Trans. Françoise Lionnet-McCumber. *Diacritics* 17, no. 3 (Fall): 39–55.

———. 1987c. *Paroles suffoquées.* Paris: Galilée.

———. 1988a. Beyond Aporia? Trans. David Macey. In *Post-Structuralist Classics*, ed. Andrew Benjamin, 7–44. New York: Routledge. Partial translation of Kofman 1983a.

———. 1988b. *The Childhood of Art.* Trans. W. Woodhull. New York: Columbia University Press. A translation of Kofman 1970.

———. 1990a. Conversions: *The Merchant of Venice* under the Sign of Saturn. Trans. Shaun Whiteside. In *Literary Theory Today*, ed. P. Collier and H. Geyer-Ryan. Cambridge: Polity Press. A translation of Kofman 1987a.

———. 1990b. *Séductions: De Sartre à Héraclite.* Paris: Galilée.

———. 1991. *Freud and Fiction.* Trans. Sarah Wykes. London: Polity. A translation of Kofman 1974.

———. 1992. *Explosion I: De l'"Ecce Homo" de Nietzsche.* Paris: Galilée.

———. 1993a. Interview avec Sarah Kofman, 22 mars 1991: Subvertir le philosophique ou Pour un supplément de jouissance. By E. Lender. *Compar(a)ison* 1: 9–26.

———. 1993b. *Nietzsche and Metaphor.* Trans. D. Large. London: Athlone Press; Stanford: Stanford University Press. A translation of Kofman 1972.

———. 1993c. *Explosion II: Les enfants de Nietzsche.* Paris: Galilée.

———. 1994a. "It's only the first step that costs." In *Speculations after Freud: Psychoanalysis, Philosophy and Culture*, ed. Sonu Shamdasani and Michael Münchow, 97–131. New York: Routledge.

———. 1994b. *Le mépris des Juifs: Nietzsche, les Juifs, l'antisémitisme.* Paris: Galilée.

———. 1995a. *L'imposture de la beauté et autres textes.* Paris: Galilée.

———. 1995b. La mort conjurée: Remarques sur *La leçon d'anatomie du docteur Nicolas Tulp*, 1632 Mauritshuis, La Haye. *La Part de l'œuil* 11 (1995): 41–45.

———. 1996. *Rue Ordener, rue Labat.* Trans. A. Smock. Lincoln: University of Nebraska Press. Original French edition: *Rue Ordener, rue Labat.* Paris: Galilée, 1994.

———. 1998a. Entretien. In Catherine Rodgers, *Le "deuxième sexe" de Simone de Beauvoir: Un héritage admiré et contesté.* Paris: L'Harmattan.

———. 1998b. *Smothered Words.* Trans. Madeleine Dobie. Evanston, IL: Northwestern University Press. A translation of Kofman 1987c.

———. 1998c. *Socrates: Fictions of a Philosopher.* Trans. Catherine Porter. Ithaca, NY: Cornell University Press.

———. 1999. Mirror and Oneiric Mirages: Plato, Precursor of Freud. *Harvard Review of Philosophy* 7: 4–14.

Kristeva, Julia. 1984. *Revolution in Poetic Language.* Trans Margaret Waller. New York: Columbia University Press.

Lacan, Jacques. 1977. Subversion of the subject and dialectic of desire. *Ecrits.* Trans. Alan Sheridan. New York: W. W. Norton.

Lacoue-Labarthe, Philippe. 1978. La césure du speculatif. In Friedrich Hölderlin, *L'Antigone de Sophocle*, ed. and trans. Lacoue-Labarthe, 183–223. Paris: Christian Bourgois.

Lacoue-Labarthe, Philippe and Jean-Luc Nancy. 1981. Le peuple juif ne rêve pas. In *La Psychanalyse est-elle une histoire juive?* 57–92. Collected texts presented at a 1980 colloquium in Montpellier. Paris: Editions du Seuil.

Laplanche, Jean. 1976. *Life and Death in Psychoanalysis.* Trans. Jeffrey Mehlman. Baltimore: Johns Hopkins University Press.

Laplanche, Jean and J.-B. Pontalis 1973. *The Language of Psycho-analysis.* Trans. D. Nicholson-Smith. New York: W. W. Norton.

Large, Duncan. 1995. Double "Whaam!" Sarah Kofman on *Ecce Homo*. *German Life and Letters* 48, no. (4) (October): 441–62.

———. 1999. Kofman's Hoffmann. In Deutscher and Oliver, 67–83, 242–45.

Nancy, Jean-Luc. 1999. Foreword: Run, Sarah! Trans. Paul Patton. In Deutscher and Oliver, viii–xvi.

Nietzsche, Friedrich. 1966. *Beyond Good and Evil.* Trans. Walter Kaufmann. New York: Random House.

———. 1967. *On the Genealogy of Morals.* Trans. Walter Kaufmann and R. J. Hollingdale. New York: Random House.

———. 1974. *The Gay Science.* Trans. Walter Kaufmann. New York: Random House.

———. 1980. *Werke: Kritische Studienausgabe.* Ed. Giorgio Colli and Mazzino Montinari. Bd. 6. Berlin: Walter de Gruyter.

———. 1981. *Briefwechsel: Kritische Gesamtausgabe.* Ed. Giorgio Colli and Mazzino Montinari. Abt. 3, Bd. 1. Berlin: Walter de Gruyter.

———. 1982. *The Viking Portable Nietzsche.* Trans. and ed. Walter Kaufmann. New York: Viking Press.

———. 1986. *Human, All Too Human.* Trans. R. J. Hollingdale. Cambridge: Cambridge University Press.

———. 1992. *Ecce Homo: How One Becomes What One Is.* Trans. R. J. Hollingdale, 2nd ed. Harmondsworth, England: Penguin.

———. 2000. *The Birth of Tragedy from the Spirit of Music.* Trans. Douglas Smith. New York: Oxford University Press.

Ovid. 1993. *The Metamorphoses of Ovid.* Trans. Allen Mandelbaum. New York: Harcourt, Brace.

Plato. 1961. *Greater Hippias.* Trans. Benjamin Jowett. In *Plato: Collected Dialogues*, ed. Edith Hamilton and Huntington Cairns, 1534–50. Princeton, NJ: Princeton University Press.

Proust, F. 1997. Impasses et passes. In *Sarah Kofman*, 5–10. Paris: Les Cahiers du Grif, Descartes & Cie.

Rose, Jacqueline. 1990. Dora: Fragment of an Analysis. In Bernheimer and Kahane 1990, 128–48.

Rousseau, Jean-Jacques. 1962. *Julie ou la nouvelle Héloïse*, vol. 2 of *Œuvres complètes.* Paris: Gallimard, Bibliothèque de la Pléiade.

Saghafi, Kas. 2001. Sarah Kofman. In Jacques Derrida, *The Work of Mourning*, eds. Pascale-Anne Brault and Michael Naas, 165–7. Chicago: University of Chicago Press.

———. 2003. Sarah Kofman. In Jacques Derrida, *Chaque fois unique, la fin du monde*, eds. Pascale-Anne Brault and Michael Naas, 379–81. Paris: Galilée.

Sartre, J-.P. 1967. *Words.* Trans. Irene Clephane. Harmondsworth: Penguin.

———. 1970. *Anti-Semite and Jew.* Trans. G. J. Becker. New York: Schocken Books.

Schrift. A. 1990. *Nietzsche and the Question of Interpretation: Between Hermeneutics and Deconstruction.* New York: Routledge.

———. 1999. Kofman, Nietzsche, and the Jews. In Deutscher and Oliver 1999, 205–18.

———. 2000. Nietzsche *for* Democracy? *Nietzsche-Studien* 29:220–33.

———. 2002. Response to Don Dombowsky. *Nietzsche-Studien* 31:291–97.

Stoller, Robert. 1984. *Sex and Gender: The Development of Masculinity.* 2 vols. London: Karnac.

Taylor, S. 1990. *Left-Wing Nietzscheans: The Politics of German Expressionism, 1910–1920.* Berlin: Walter de Gruyter.

Thomas, R. H. 1983. *Nietzsche in German Politics and Society, 1890–1918.* Manchester: Manchester University Press.

Wilde, O. 1992. *The Picture of Dorian Gray.* New York: Random House.

Yovel, Y. 1998. *Dark Riddle: Hegel, Nietzsche, and the Jews.* London: Polity Press.

Contributors

Tina Chanter is professor of philosophy at DePaul University. She is author of *Ethics of Eros: Irigaray's Rereading of the Philosophers* (Routledge, 1995), *Time, Death and the Feminine: Levinas with Heidegger* (Stanford University Press, 2001), and *Gender* (Continuum Press, 2006). Her book, *The Picture of Abjection: Film, Fetish and the Nature of Difference*, is forthcoming with Indiana University Press. She is editor of *Feminist Interpretations of Emmanuel Levinas* (Pennsylvania State University Press, 2001), and coeditor (with Ewa Ziarek) of *Revolt, Affect Collectivity: The Unstable Boundaries of Kristeva's Polis* (SUNY, 2005). She is also editor of the Gender Theory series at the State University of New York Press.

Pleshette DeArmitt is assistant professor of philosophy at the University of Memphis, and researches in the areas of twentieth-century French philosophy, feminism, and psychoanalysis. She has published articles on Kristeva, Kofman, and Derrida in journals such as *Research in Phenomenology*, *Philosophy Today*, and *The Southern Journal of Philosophy*. Most recently, she edited a special memorial issue of *Epoché* (Spring 2006) on Jacques Derrida.

Penelope Deutscher is an associate professor in philosophy at Northwestern University. Her publications include: *Yielding Gender: Feminism, Deconstruction and the History of Philosophy* (Routledge, 1997) and *A Politics of Impossible Difference: The Later Work of Luce Irigaray* (Cornell University Press, 2002). She coedited (with Kelly Oliver) *Enigmas: Essays on Sarah Kofman* (Cornell University Press, 1999) and (with Françoise Collin) *Repenser le politique: L'apport du féminisme* (Cahiers du Grif, 2004).

Duncan Large is professor of German at Swansea University. He has translated Kofman's *Nietzsche and Metaphor* (Stanford University Press, 1993) and coedited (with Keith Ansell Pearson) *The Nietzsche Reader* (Blackwell, 2006). He is the author of *Nietzsche and Proust: A Comparative Study* (Clarendon Press, 2001) and is currently completing a monograph entitled *Nietzsche's Renaissance Figures*.

Michael Naas is professor of philosophy at DePaul University in Chicago. He is the author of *Turning: From Persuasion to Philosophy* (Humanities Press,

1995) and *Taking on the Tradition: Jacques Derrida and the Legacies of Deconstruction* (Stanford University Press, 2003). He is the coeditor of Jacques Derrida's *The Work of Mourning* (University of Chicago Press, 2001) and the cotranslator, with Pascale-Anne Brault, of several works by Derrida, including *The Other Heading* (Indiana University Press, 1992), *Memoirs of the Blind* (University of Chicago Press, 1993), *Adieu—to Emmanuel Levinas* (Stanford University Press, 1999), and *Rogues* (Stanford University Press, 2005).

Alan D. Schrift is the F. Wendell Miller Professor of Philosophy and founding director of the Grinnell College Center for the Humanities. He is the author of three books: *Twentieth Century French Philosophy: Key Themes and Thinkers* (Blackwell Publishers, 2005), *Nietzsche's French Legacy: A Genealogy of Poststructuralism* (Routledge, 1995), and *Nietzsche and the Question of Interpretation: Between Hermeneutics and Deconstruction* (Routledge, 1990). Schrift has also edited five collections on a variety of topics: *Modernity and the Problem of Evil* (Indiana University Press, 2005), *Why Nietzsche Still? Reflections on Drama, Culture, and Politics* (University of California Press, 2000), *The Logic of the Gift: Toward an Ethic of Generosity* (Routledge, 1997), *The Hermeneutic Tradition: From Ast to Ricoeur* (State University of New York Press, 1990), and *Transforming the Hermeneutic Context: From Nietzsche to Nancy* (State University of New York Press, 1990).

Ann Smock is a professor of French literature at the University of California, Berkeley. She is the translator of two books by Maurice Blanchot—*The Space of Literature* and *The Writing of the Disaster* (University of Nebraska Press, 1982 and 1986, respectively)—and of Sarah Kofman's memoir *Rue Ordener, rue Labat* (University of Nebraska Press, 1996). She is the author of *Double Dealing* (University of Nebraska Press, 1986)—essays on Giraudoux, Nabokov, Klossowski, and Kafka—and of *What Is There to Say?* (University of Nebraska Press, 2003), on Blanchot, Herman Melville, Louis-René des Forêts, Paulhan and Beckett. An example of her interest in contemporary poetry is an essay, "Cloudy Roubaud," published in *Representations*, no. 86 (2004).

Index